Erika Knight

Simple Color Knitting

A Complete How-to-Knit-with-Color Workshop with 20 Projects

Photography by Yuki Sugiura

St. Martin's Griffin
New York

Publishing director Jane O'Shea
Commissioning editor Lisa Pendreigh
Editorial assistant Harriet Butt
Pattern checker Sally Harding
Creative director Helen Lewis
Art director and Designer Claire Peters
Photographer Yuki Sugiura
Stylist Holly Bruce
Model Chinh Hoang
Illustrator Claire Peters
Production director Vincent Smith
Production controller Stephen Lang

Printed in China. For information, address
St. Martin's Press, 175 Fifith Avenue, New
York, N.Y. 10010.

www.stmartins.com

Library of Congress Cataloging-in-
Publication Data Available Upon Request

ISBN 978-1-250-03909-5

First U.S. Edition: September 2015

10 9 8 7 6 5 4 3 2 1

Our books may be purchased in bulk
for promotional, educational, or
business use. Please contact your local
bookseller or the Macmillan Corporate
and Premium Sales Department at (800)
221-7945, extension 5442, or by e-mail
at MacmillanSpecialMarkets@macmillan.com.

Project Workshops 58

Introduction

Color evokes emotion. Color affects our senses. Color is a gauge of our mood. Color conjures memories.

I have been designing palettes of color for the fashion industry, and more specifically for knitwear and printed textiles, for much of my life. My fine art training instilled in me a love for the language of color and its many dialects. Personally, my own color palette tends toward natural shades and monochromes as a base with bright pops of color to add energy and life.

Using color within knitting to create interesting stitches, patterns, and textiles is one of the most exciting aspects of the craft. This book is a glimpse into my creative process; how I look at, select, and use color. Rather than being an exhaustive tome on color science or every color knitting technique, instead *Simple Color Knitting* is my personal view on color. This book is more of a "workbox," designed to inspire a diverse, versatile, and "big brush" approach to color.

Simple Color Knitting is about ways of incorporating color in your knitting, with practical advice from techniques of plying, phasing, slipping stitches, stranding, color blocking, embroidering, and embellishing to more expressive approaches. Throughout this book the twenty projects build in skill level and provide a base to practice, experiment, and create with color. My hope it that it will inspire confidence in your own selections of color and methods of using it.

We must hold on to our individuality through our creative endeavors, most especially our hand knits. Key to this is the "handcrafted." A craft that comes from the hand is for me the greatest form of creativity; honest, authentic, and personal. Show your true colors. Add color to your knitting.

erika knight

Skill levels

In reality, all the projects in this book are unashamedly simple—that's my style. However, each project has been attributed with a skill level in accordance with the Craft Yarn Council of America's rating system in order to let you know what techniques you are mastering.

BEGINNER

1 Beginner Projects For first-time knitters using basic knit and purl stitches. Minimal shaping.

EASY

2 Easy Projects Using basic stitches, repetitive stitch patterns, simple color changes, and simple shaping and finishing.

INTERMEDIATE

3 Intermediate Projects With a variety of stitches, such as basic cables and lace, simple intarsia, knitting-in-the-round techniques, mid-level shaping and finishing.

EXPERIENCED

4 Experienced Projects Using advanced techniques and stitches, such as short rows, Fair Isle, more intricate intarsia, cables, lace patterns, and numerous color changes.

Inspiration

A ripe fig, a slick of oil on water, a patch of lichen on a rock, weathered paint on a wooden table. Inspiration cannot be prescriptive, it is instinctive and individual. The ways in which you may respond to that inspiration are many and varied, but finding it can sometimes seem a daunting task. Eliminate the white page. Take a walk. Visit a gallery. Go to a market. It's all about looking. Learn from what you see, trusting your eye and your judgement.

Source. Collect. Collate. Photograph. Play. Record. Draw. Paint. Crayon. Cut out. Alter. Photocopy. Reduce. Enlarge. Distort. Repeat.

The perfect colorway for a throw or a muffler may already exist within your favorite image, torn from a magazine and pinned to your noticeboard. Match the colors in that favorite image, painting, postcard, or fabric to shades of yarn and wind off those onto a strip of cardboard. While I was at art school, a tutor once said to me, "It always comes back to landscape." When I am in in need of inspiration, it invariably does.

There are simple ways of producing personal, colorful, and creative designs from the many and plentiful sources that fill our lives and experiences. I hope that the projects in this book will inspire and encourage you to be brave with color, and to use your own personal response to colors in your knitting. There are no rights and wrongs with color, only an understanding of how to use it to maximum effect.

Use the basics of the color wheel as shown over the next pages, then invent and experiment with your own palettes:

Red—lifeforce, physical, passion, festivity, dominance
Blue—sky and sea, workers, eternity, uniform, change, tranquility, new beginnings, durable, trust, loyalty
Yellow—energy, power, precious, sacred, optimism, youth
Green—nature, life, harmony, calming, everlasting, faith
Pink—romance, fidelity, compassion, action, confidence
Purple—regal, mystery, enlightenment, comfort, nostalgia
Orange—ambition, generosity, vibrancy, happiness, energy
Black—timeless, practical, spiritual, urban, confident
White—pure, integrity, clarity, spiritual, fresh, peace
Naturals—grounded, stable, secure, the perfect foil to accent or play with color; a base on which to build.

color theory

Explaining our response to color is as much about quantifying an emotional reaction as it is explaining an exact science.

Johannes Itten, a prominent teacher at the Bauhaus, produced the "color wheel" in its most recognizable form. He used blocks of primary, secondary, and tertiary colors to form a wheel of twelve segments. Visually, each of the segments represents a color and the wheel as a whole represents their circular relationship.

The principle of the color wheel is that there are three PRIMARY colors: red, yellow, and blue. They are primary as they exist alone and cannot be made up of any other color.

Mixing primary colors in equal proportions creates SECONDARY colors; red and yellow create orange, blue and yellow create green, and red and blue make violet.

The remaining six segments on the color wheel show the TERTIARY colors, which result from mixing adjacent and secondary colors in a ratio of 2:1 to produce red-orange, yellow-orange, yellow-green, blue-green, blue-purple, and red-purple.

Black and white are not strictly classified as colors, and do not appear on the color wheel.

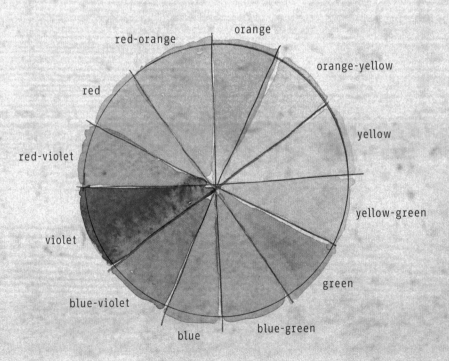

Whether you are selecting colors for the striped blanket or the tweed stitch scarf, the simplicity of the color wheel is a fun tool for devising a colorway for a project.

On the following pages, four of the most useful ways of employing the color wheel to create a colorway are explained: complementary or "opposites attract"; analogous or "next-to's"; split complementary or "triangular"; monochromatic or "ombré."

red

blue

yellow

Primary

purple

orange

green

Secondary

orange

light orange

fuchsia

light green

light purple

light blue

Tertiary

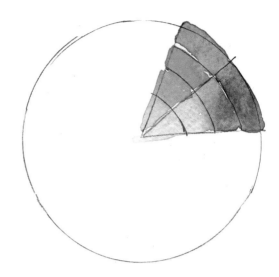

Opposites attract

Any two hues positioned directly opposite each other on the color wheel are considered to be complementary colors. This always creates a dynamic energy, which is why I refer to them as "opposites attract," and has great impact when used in moderation in a design. Blue with orange, red with green, and yellow with purple, for example. When they are placed next to each other they make the other appear more intense and brighter. That's because, being opposite, one color is always cool and the other is always warm with the greatest contrast.

I have used this simple color principle in another way for the Faux Sheepskin Throw (see page 60). The natural wool "fur" yarn in vibrant purple is styled with a brilliant yellow upholstered chair, creating a dynamic focus for a living room.

Next-to's

Colors that sit next to each other on the color wheel are known as analogous, or as I simply call them "next-to's." Basically, this color scheme features three or more hues, which are positioned next to each other on the color wheel. Just choose any color on the wheel as your main color, then simply add the two or three colors next to it on either side of it. They all share similarities at their source and will easily harmonize. Next-to color schemes are often found in nature, and well, if it works in the natural world, it should look good on a bit of knitted fabric.

You may have a few balls of the main color in your stash from a bargain or just "had to have it" moment at the yarn store. So this is a good way to extend into a bigger project.

This does create a simple and successful colorway. These bright hues do work together and create a harmonious effect and are fab for kids knits, but maybe use a softer tone of one or two of the colors if a little more sophistication is required. Make sure you have enough contrast when choosing an analogous color scheme. Maybe choose one color to dominate, a second to support. The third color is used (along with black, white, or gray) as an accent.

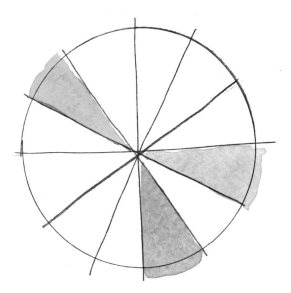

Triangular

A split complementary color scheme is made up of three hues. First, pick your main color. Next, go directly across to its complementary color on the color wheel. Don't pick this, but select the two colors either side of the complementary color. For example, if you start with red, the color opposite is green, but don't use this, instead use the yellow-green and blue-green either side.

Wherever you begin, there will always be at least one tertiary color in your selection. As tertiary colors are blends, the final palette will be sophisticated with subtle mixes.

I organize my yarn stash in groups according to color. The differing weights and textures add another dimension and aid the process of design. There are basic lessons to learn from color theory, but do not assume that colors will always work together exactly as intended; go with the flow, experiment, and be pleasantly surprised. All too often, selecting even a single shade for a project is tricky, let alone choosing three or more colors to work together. The one thing I have learned along the way is that a color can look very different when combined with others. It is always essential to "swatch" up colors as they look different when knitted up as opposed to in the ball or hank.

Hand dyes
Your color inspiration may come all in one hank of yarn, where the hand dyer has done the work for you. Beautiful contrasts, harmonies, and tonal effects can be achieved in a single continuous thread of multi-colored or hand-dyed yarn. Use it on its own or to add further depth to a Fair Isle as the background to accent colors. Alternatively, use stitch patterns that break the straight row and create further color effects, such as a 'slip stitch'.

Tones

Black and white are not strictly classified as colors. They do not appear on the color wheel. But black and white used simply together, I find, give great energy. I always use this color combination in every collection. Black and white is always classic, always coveted.

Adding black or white to a color will make a range of tints, tones, and shades. If a color is made lighter by adding white, the result is called a tint. If black is added, the darker version is called a shade. And if gray is added the result will be a different tone.

My personal favorite project in this book is monochromatic—using different tints, shades, or tones of one color together in one project. This is a very comfortable and safe choice. I have taken three fabulous hand dyes in blue, ranging from a dark indigo shade through a hue of denim blue to a tint of light chambray to create a further ombré effect by further plying the yarns and phasing the colors to knit a simple garter stitch throw and create a dip-dyed effect (see page 68).

The monochromatic color scheme creates quite a sophisticated effect, maybe a beautiful variation to a solid color knit and, indeed, many variations, obvious and some subtle, can be achieved from just one color in this way.

tint   hue   shade

color techniques

Plying & Phasing

Plying and phasing are two very simple techniques to inject color into your knitting. By using two or more balls of different shades of yarn, but held together and worked with as if they were one yarn, you can create some simple yet stunning color effects.

Plying

Play around with different effects when plying together yarns to create energetic and individual effects. Try using a bulky yarn plied together with a strand of fine yarn. Combine a mat yarn, such as a cotton, with shiny yarn, such as mercerized cotton or viscose.

Create strong color contrasts or more subtle effects to mimic the appearance of hand-dyed yarns.

To estimate the amount of yarn required for a project, knit up a small swatch, then unravel it and measure the length of yarn to guesstimate the amount of yarn needed for the size of the finished pieces.

Take care not to "split" the yarn. Make sure you always work the strands together when working a stitch.

Take one strand of color A + one strand of color B and use them both together as one yarn.

Phasing

Use a sticky note to mark the actual row you are working on to avoid any confusion.

An ombré or phased effect can be created by using three or more colors of yarn.

Stripes in stockinette stitch make a clean line on the knit side and a "broken" stripe on the purl side.

On garter stitch stripes I especially like the "wrong side" of the fabric.

Rib stitch stripes create a lively textile enhanced by the 'color change' stitch peeking through.

Personally I favor odd-row stripes and even single row stripes, although this results in more yarn ends to weave in.

Striping

Stripes may be any width and color sequence you like: even or odd numbers of rows, the same color sequence repeated, alternating widths or colors—the choice is yours. Horizontal stripes are the easiest way of working with two or more colors.

Take color inspiration from a postcard of a favorite painting, ceramic, or home textile—even a magazine cutting. Match the chosen colors from the inspirational image to yarns, then wind lengths of each yarn around a strip of cardboard to create pleasing color combinations and proportions (see pages 8–9). Referring to the inspiration strip, knit an individual textile imitating the proportions of color and stripes.

If working wide stripes, cut the yarn at the end of each stripe. If working thinner or even-row stripes, the yarn can be carried up the side to avoid extra darning or weaving in later

It's easy to work odd-row stripes on double-pointed needles or a circular needle.

Joining a new color at the beginning of a row

1 When changing color or joining in a new ball—on the row before you need the new color, work to the last stitch.

2 Taking the end of the new color, use it together with the yarn in work to work the last stitch, creating a "double stitch."

3 On the first stitch of the next row, work the double stitch as one stitch with just the end of the new color. This will securely "anchor" your new yarn and not create unsightly knots or bumps.

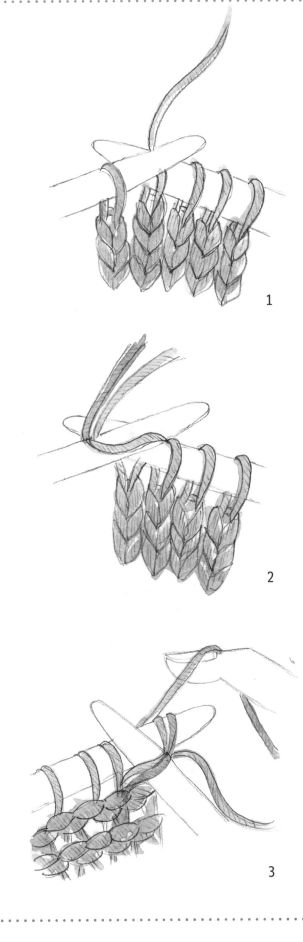

1

2

3

Stranding

Fair Isling or Fair Isle is a general term used for multicolored stockinette stitch patterns. Authentic Fair Isles are very colorful with small motifs, often personal to the knitter, repeated across a row, using only two colors— one always carried at the back of the fabric, thus creating a double-thick fabric perfect for the cold Northern European climate where these were first created.

There are two methods used when working Fair Isle patterns—stranding the unused yarn all across the wrong side of the knitting, and weaving the two yarns together on the wrong side to avoid long loops of yarn.

Stranding with one hand involves dropping one yarn after use, then picking up another and carrying it across the back of the work. It is important not to twist the yarns in the changeover between colors.

On a right-side (knit) row Using the first color, knit three stitches. Drop the yarn and pick up the second color, carrying it over the dropped yarn, and knit three stitches. Drop the second color.

Pick up the first color from underneath the second and bring it across the back of the last three knitted stitches. Knit the next three stitches, being careful not to pull the yarn too tight.

On a wrong-side (purl) row Using the first color, purl three stitches. Drop the yarn and pick up the second color, carrying it across the last three stitches over the top of the dropped color. Purl three stitches. Drop the second color.

Pick up the first color from underneath the second, bring it across, and purl three stitches. Keep the stitches spread out along the right needle to avoid puckering.

Using the stranding technique with two hands is faster than using just one, since the yarns do not need to be dropped between color changes. Hold one color over the index finger of the left hand as for the continental knitting method, and the other according to the style in which you knit in the right hand.

On a right-side (knit) row * Using the first color, which is held in the right hand, knit three stitches.

Using your left hand, bring the second color across the back of the work, over the top of the first yarn and knit the next three stitches in the continental style. Repeat from * to end.

On a wrong-side (purl) row Hold the first color over the left index finger and the second yarn in your right hand. Purl three stitches in the second color, carrying it over the last three stitches.

Using the first yarn and the continental method, purl the next three stitches.

Weaving

If a color needs to be carried across the back of the work over more than three stitches, it will need to be caught or woven in. It is best to do this every second or third stitch, since weaving on every stitch can distort the shape of the knitted stitch and weaving too infrequently creates loops. As with stranding, weaving can be done using either the one-handed or two-handed method.

On a right-side (knit) row Work to the point where the second color needs to be caught in. Bring the second color up from under the one in use and over the right needle and your left index finger from right to left.

Using the right needle, knit the stitch, dropping the stitch and the carried yarn from the left needle as you do so. Hold the carried yarn in place at the back of the work, using your left index finger, and continue to knit using the first color.

On a wrong-side (purl) row Work to the point where the second color needs to be caught in. Bring the second color up from under the one in use and around the right needle from right to left, anchoring it in place with your left thumb at the front of the work.

Using the right needle, purl the next stitch, taking care not to take the carried color through the stitch. Continue to purl following the pattern.

Color Blocking

With color blocking any number of
colors can be used in a single row
to create a placed motif or picture.
There is no need to strand or weave
on the wrong side of the knitting, as
individual colors are introduced as and
when they are required within the row
using a separate ball of yarn to create
a single fabric.

Changing yarn using the color-block (intarsia) method

When knitting using several colors across
a row, organize the yarns into small balls
or "bobbins"—small windings of individual
yarns. To work out how much yarn you will
need, calculate the number of stitches in that
specific area then twist the yarn around the
knitting needle that number of times, adding
a small amount more for sewing in the ends.
Once you have measured out the correct
amount of yarn, either wind it into a small
bobbin by hand or wrap it around a store-
bought bobbin.

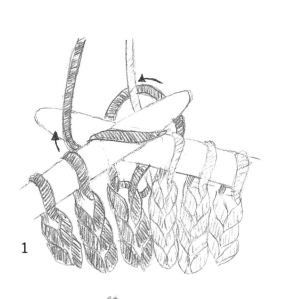

1 To change to a new color on a knit row, work
up to the color change. Drop the old color. Pick
up the new color from under the old color and
knit to the next color change.

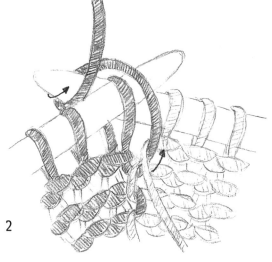

2 On a purl row, work up to the color change.
Drop the old color. Pick up the new color
from under the old color and purl to the next
color change.

In effect, you are "twisting" the two colors
around each other to link them together. Be
careful not to overtwist the yarn or the fabric
will not lie flat. The object is to link together
the two separate color sections so that they
form a single fabric.

Working from charts

Color patterns are often worked from charts and the colors are indicated by either colored squares or symbols within each square.

Each square represents a stitch and each row of squares represents a row of knitting. The patterns are worked in stockinette stitch, i.e. one row knit, one row purl alternately, unless otherwise stated.

Read the knit rows (usually odd-numbered) from right to left and read the purl rows (usually even-numbered) from left to right (unless otherwise instructed by the pattern). Continue to work on this principle until the design is completed.

Square Motif
- use a separate ball of yarn for each area of color

26 stitches

Embroidering

Duplicate stitch (or Swiss darning) is a form of embroidery made to look like knit stitches. Using a blunt-tipped sewing needle and yarn, you can sew small areas of color over the top of knitted stitches to add decorative detail without having to use the tricky technique of knitting with multiple colors.

Take inspiration from fabrics—simply photocopy the fabric, reduce or enlarge the image as required and trace it onto graph paper. Use needlepoint designs as inspiration, too.

Adapt the outline of the design you have chosen to fit the squares or photocopy directly onto knitters chart paper, simplifying the areas of "tones" of color. Remember that each square on the graph or chart paper represents one stitch.

Once your design is on the chart, follow it to duplicate stitch the motif on top of your knitting.

To knit each of the colored stitches that make up the rose motif on the Plaid Rose Pillow (see pages 138–141) would be incredibly difficult and challenge even the most proficient knitter. I think you get a far better result by embroidering the odd highlight color over a base color. But do make sure when you are working duplicate stitches over the top of the knitted stitches, not to pull the embroidered stitches too tight as this will pucker the fabric.

Mark the section you are going to start embroidering with pins (1).

2

Thread a large blunt-tipped needle with yarn of the same ply as the background. Secure by working two or three stitches on top of one another at the back of the first stitch. Insert the needle from the back to the front, through the base of the first stitch. Thread the needle from right to left under the two vertical loops of the same stitch, but one row above (2).

Gently pull the yarn through; a stitch is formed covering the right-hand vertical top loop of the knitted stitch. Then re-insert the needle ino the base of the stitch to be covered, and then out to the front again through the base of the next stitch to the left (3).

3

Pull the yarn through; one duplicate stitch is now complete. Do not pull the yarn too tightly; the darning must be the same gauge as the background.

To complete the first line of a block of color, continue working from right to left along a row for the number of stitches required. The stitches should all be flat and even.

It is easier to work the second and alternate rows if you turn the knitting upside down. This is so that the stitches are always worked in the same direction.

1

Slipping Stitches

Slipping stitches is one of the simplest ways of putting color into your knitting. If you are concerned about working with more than one color at a time, this is the technique for you as only one color is used in each row.

The tweed stitch used in the Muffler Scarf on page 92 is a good example of a simple slip-stitch color pattern. It is slow to knit but produces a flat woven-like fabric. You may find it easier to work this stitch on a larger size needle than the one suggested in the pattern.

The tweed stitch also creates a versatile and attractive double-sided textile. Worked in three colors, it requires a dark (A), medium (B), and a light (C) color to give a good contrast. My favorite combination is simply black, gray, and ecru (light fawn).

Tip To try out the tweed stitch, cast on an odd number of stitches and work the stitch following the instructions on page 93. If you aren't certain which color to use next when working the stitch stitch, pick up the color at the beginning of the needles, two rows below the "working" stitches.

Slipping a stitch purlwise

When a slip-stitch color pattern simply instructs you to slip one or more stitches, without specifying how you should do this, it means that the stitches are to be slipped purlwise.

To slip a stitch purlwise on a knit row, first insert the tip of the right needle, from right to left, through the front loop of the next stitch on the left needle. Keep the yarn at the back of the work unless your instructions state otherwise. You will have inserted the right needle as if you were about to work a purl stitch, but instead, you slip the stitch onto the right needle. The slipped stitch now sits on the right needle with the right side of the loop at the front, like the worked stitches next to it.

Slip a stitch on a purl row in the same way, but keep the yarn at the front of the work unless your instructions state otherwise.

Finishing

When all the knitted pieces are done,
take time to finish...

Ends

To sew in yarn ends, use a blunt-tipped needle
to "weave" each end in separately across the
knitting on the wrong side (never along the
edges) for about four stitches, then back one to
two stitches to hold the end firmly in place.

This technique is especially good for cotton,
linens, and hemps as due to their "plant" nature
they are nonelastic and tend to unravel.

Picking up stitches

You may sometimes need to pick up and knit
stitches along the edge of your knitting, for
example to add on a knitted edging. To pick up
stitches evenly, divide the edge into regular
sections with pins placed at right angles to the
edge, then divide the total number of stitches
required by the number of sections. Pick up that
number of stitches between each pin.

Along row ends
Use pins to mark the row ends along the selvage,
evenly spacing the pins at the end of every four
rows, as shown here. Pick up and knit three
stitches between each pair of pins, inserting
the needle into the center of the edge stitch,
wrapping the yarn around the tip of the needle
and drawing the yarn through to create a loop on
the needle.

Along a curved edge
On most armhole borders and neckbands you will
need to pick up stitches along a curved edge. As
a general rule, pick up one stitch in each bound-
off stitch and three for every four row ends. For
a smooth edge, do not pick up corner stitches on
stepped decreases.

Invisible seam

Invisible seams are used to sew all side and sleeve seams, or where a flat seam with no bulk is required.

With the right side of both pieces facing you, secure the yarn to the edge of one piece. Take the needle across to the opposite edge, pick up the equivalent stitch on this piece, pull the yarn through; take the needle back to the first edge, returning the needle through the hole of the previous stitch, then pick up the next stitch and pull the yarn through.

Continue in this way picking up and pulling together stitch to stitch (row for row) along the length of the seam.

Once you have mastered this, you will never look back.

Backstitch seam

A backstitch seam is used where a firm edge is required to hold the shape, such as a set-in sleeve, or to give strength at any point where the garment may take extra strain. It can also be used as a decorative feature of the design, for pillows, etc.

Place the pieces with the right sides together. Work along the wrong side of the fabric one stitch from the edge.

Secure the yarn and work from right to left. With the needle at the back of the work move along to the left the length of one knitted stitch, bring the needle through fabric to front and pull the yarn through. Take the needle from left to right across front of work to the end of last stitch, insert the needle through the fabric to the back of the work, and pull the yarn through. Continue in this way.

Blocking

The process of pinning and pressing knitted pieces is called blocking and it will make your finished projects look as good as possible. First sew in the yarn ends, then steam or wet press as appropriate.

Block and pin

To block a piece of knitting, pin it out to the correct size and shape on your irongin board or a padded surface (a table covered with a folded blanket under a sheet is ideal). Pin each piece, wrong side facing up. Do not stretch or distort the fabric. Make sure all the rows run in straight lines. Check that the width and length of each piece match the measurements given on the pattern. Pin closely around the edge of each piece of knitting, placing pins at right angles to the edges.

Steam pressing

This method is used for natural yarns or those with a high wool content. Care should be taken with long-haired fibers, such as mohair and angora, or items with textured stitches, to ensure the steaming process does not mat the fibers or flatten the pattern. Check the information on the yarn label and test-press a gauge square first if you have any doubts.

Use rustproof large-headed pins to pin out each piece to its exact measurements as explained above. Lay a clean cotton cloth over your pinned knitting to protect it.

Set the iron to an appropriate heat setting for your yarn. Hold the iron close to the cotton cloth and allow the steam to permeate. Do not press the iron onto the knitted fabric. Remove the cloth and allow the knitting to dry before unpinning.

Wet pressing

This method is suitable for synthetics and fancy yarns. Pin out your knitting as for steam pressing. Wet a clean cloth and squeeze out the excess water until it is just damp. Place the cloth over your knitting and leave to dry. Remove the cloth when it is completely dry and ensure the knitted pieces are also dry before unpinning them.

swatch gallery

opposites attract

Colors on opposing sides of the color wheel (see page 12) always provide a vibrant contrast, one color is always cool while the other is always warm. When contrasting or complementary colors are adjacent they make each other appear brighter and more intense.

Worked over any number of stitches

Horizontal bands of contrasting color worked in stockinette stitch.

Worked over any number of stitches

Vertical bands of contrasting color worked in stockinette stitch using the color-blocking (intarsia) technique (see page 32).

Bright Pink + Bright Green

- *experiment with opposing colors*

Orange + Blue

- *cast on and bind off a scarf in contrasting colors*

Purple + Yellow

- *contrasting colors create energy*

Black + Neutral

- *not strictly on the color wheel but never to be ignored*

Worked over any number of stitches

Vertical bands of contrasting color worked in stockinette stitch and reverse stockinette stitch alternately using the color-blocking (intarsia) technique (see page 32).

Worked over any number of stitches

Horizontal bands of contrasting color worked in reverse stockinette stitch.

plying and phasing

Individual effects are created using two or more colors as one yarn. This "make do and mend" technique disguises any shortage when a substitute yarn is introduced.

Worked over any number of stitches, using colors A and B

Work in stockinette stitch (K 1 row, P 1 row alternately), using one end of A and one end of B held together.

Worked over any number of stitches, using colors A and B

Work in reverse stockinette stitch (P 1 row, K 1 row alternately), using one end of A and one end of B held together.

Plied Stockinette Stitch
- one strand of color A and one strand of color B held together

Plied Reverse Stockinette Stitch
- the random texture and color of the reverse side looks equally good

Worked over any number of stitches, using colors A, B, and C

Knit every row following the color sequence below:
6 rows in A
2 rows in B
2 rows in A
2 rows in B
2 rows in A
8 rows in B
2 rows in C
2 rows in B
2 rows in C
2 rows in B
7 rows in B

Ombré Garter Stitch
- creates a subtle color effect akin to hand-dyed yarns

Worked over any number of stitches, using colors A, B, and C

Knit every row following the color sequence below with the two yarn ends held together:
4 rows in A+A
5 rows in A+B
5 rows in B+B
5 rows in B+C
4 rows in C+C

Ombré Garter Stitch
- a dip-dye effect can be created using three or more colors

striping

Stripes are a simple, effective, and varied way to add interest to knitting. Stripes can be vibrant or subtle, regular or random. Use as many colors as your yarn stash or your imagination allow.

Worked over any number of stitches, using colors A and B

Row 1 (RS) Using A, knit.
Row 2 Using A, purl.
Rows 3 and 4 Rep rows 1 and 2.
Row 5 Using A, knit.
Row 6 Using B, knit.
Rep these 6 rows.

Purl Bar Stripe
- *fine purl bar stripes create subtle interest*

Even-Row Stripes
- *even-row stripes in two colors are easy to knit and always classic*

Worked over any number of stitches, using colors A and B

Row 1 (RS) Using A, knit.
Row 2 Using A, purl.
Row 3 (RS) Using B, knit.
Row 4 Using B, purl.
Rep these 4 rows.

Diagonal Stripes
- this technique always produces a square of knitting. so creating a diagonal is easy

Start with 2 stitches and work using colors A, B, and C

Using A, cast on 2 sts.
Row 1 (RS) K1, K into front and back of last st (called *inc*).
3 sts.
Row 2 K2, inc in last st. *4 sts.*
Row 3 K to last st, inc in last st. *5 sts.*
Rep row 3 until there are 32 sts on needle.
Next row K.
Next row (dec) K to last 2 sts, K2tog. *31 sts.*
Rep last row until 26 sts rem.
Cont to dec as set, working stripes as follows:
2 rows in C
2 rows in A
4 rows in B
2 rows in A
2 rows in C
Using A, cont to dec as set until 2 sts rem.
Next row K2tog and fasten off.

Multicolor Stripes
- vary the row size of stripes to create an individual pattern

Worked over any number of stitches, using five colors— A, B, C, D, and E

Beg with a P row, work in St st stripes as follows:
*3 rows in A
2 rows in B
2 rows in C
2 rows in B
[1 row in D, 1 row in E] 7 times
1 row in D
2 rows in B
2 rows in C
2 rows in B
3 rows in A
Rep from *.

slipping stitches

In slip-stitch color patterns one color is used in each row and stitches are slipped (purlwise) to take the color over two rows (see page 36).

Worked over a multiple of 2 sts + 1 st extra, using colors A and B

Row 1 (RS) Using A, K1, *sl 1, K1; rep from * to end.
Row 2 Using A, K1, *yf, sl 1, yb, K1; rep from * to end.
Row 3 Using B, K2, *sl 1, K1; rep from * to last st, K1.
Row 4 Using B, K2, *yf, sl 1, yb, K1; rep from * to last st, K1.
Rep these 4 rows.

Worked over a multiple of 6 sts + 2 sts extra, using colors A, B, C, and D

Row 1 (RS) Using A, K.
Row 2 Using A, P.
Row 3 Using B, K2, *sl 4, K2; rep from * to end.
Row 4 Using B, P3, sl 2, *P4, sl 2; rep from * to last 3 sts, P3.
Rows 5 and 6 Using B, rep rows 1 and 2.
Row 7 Using C, K1, sl 2, K2, *sl 4, K2; rep from * to last 3 sts, sl 2, K1.
Row 8 Using C, P1, sl 1, P4, *sl 2, P4; rep from * to last 2 sts, sl 1, P1.
Rows 9 and 10 Using C, rep rows 1 and 2.
Rows 11 and 12 Using D, rep rows 3 and 4.
Rows 13 and 14 Using D, rep rows 1 and 2.
Rows 15 and 16 Using A, rep rows 7 and 8.
Rep these 16 rows.

Seed Slip Stitch
– this stitch works well for a pillow as it is firm with straight edges

Slip Stitch Diamonds
– a favorite stitch for its vintage look. I call it "Cheat's Fair Isle"

Slip Stitch Rib
- a nonelastic rib effect often used in Fair Isle sweaters

Worked over a multiple of 2 sts + 1 st extra, using colors A and B

Foundation row 1 (RS) Using A, K.
Foundation row 2 Using A, P.
Row 1 Using B, K1, *sl 1, K1; rep from * to end.
Row 2 Using B, P1, *sl 1, P1; rep from * to end.
Row 3 Using A, K2, sl 1, *K1, sl 1; rep from * to last 2 sts, K2.
Row 4 Using A, K2, sl 1, *P1, sl 1; rep from * to last 2 sts, P2.
Rep these 4 rows.

Tweed Stitch
- play with colors to see how they recede or dominate

Worked over any number of stitches, using colors A, B, and C

Set-up row (WS) Using A, P.
Row 1 (RS) Using B, K1, *yf, sl 1, yb, K1; rep from * to end.
Row 2 Using C, K1, P1, *yb, sl 1, yf, P1; rep from * to last st, K1.
Row 3 Using A, rep row 1.
Row 4 Using B, rep row 2.
Row 5 Using C, rep row 1.
Row 6 Using A, rep row 2.
Rep rows 1–6.

stranding

Created by stranding, where two colors are used in a single row, these patterns follow the color sequences given in the charts. Drop the color not in use and allow it to strand loosely across the back of the work.

Worked over any number of stitches, using colors A and B

Knit and purl alternate rows using the color as indicated on the chart on page 101.

Houndstooth Pattern
- a classic pattern and a firm favorite

Worked over an even number of stitches, using colors A and B (but vary the colours you use for A and B if desired as shown here)

Every row [K1, P1] to end.

For two-color rib, use one color for knit and one color for purl on row 1, keeping the same colors in the same stitches on subsequent rows to make vertical stripes, and always carrying the yarn on the wrong side of the fabric.

Bicolor Rib Pattern
- change the colors often to create an interesting textile with pronounced purl stitches

Worked over any number of stitches, using six colors—A, B, C, D, E, and F

Knit all RS (odd-numbered) rows and purl all WS (odd-numbered) rows, using the colors as indicated on the chart.

Reading from a chart Read knit (RS) rows from right to left and read purl (WS) rows from left to right.

Fair Isle Pattern
- endless colorways are possible with traditional patterns; pastels are an especially fresh alternative

☐	A
▨	B
☐	C
▨	D
▨	E
■	F

pattern repeat = 20 sts

color block motifs

With color blocking, any number of colors can be used in a single row to create a placed motif or picture (see page 32).

Worked over any number of stitches, using colors A and B

Knit all RS (odd-numbered) rows and purl all WS (even-numbered) rows, using the colors as indicated on the chart.

Reading from a chart Read knit (RS) rows from right to left and read purl (WS) rows from left to right.

When working large areas of color, use separate lengths or small balls of yarn for each area of color and twist the strands of yarn at the back of the work when changing colors to avoid a hole.

Square Motif
- experiment with the same color square motif but placed on different backgrounds

□ A
■ B

26 stitches

Worked over any number of stitches, using colors A and B

Knit all RS (odd-numbered) rows and purl all WS (even-numbered) rows, using the colors as indicated on the chart.

Reading from a chart Read knit (RS) rows from right to left and read purl (WS) rows from left to right.

When working large areas of color, use separate lengths or small balls of yarn for each area of color and twist the strands of yarn at the back of the work when changing colors to avoid a hole.

Checkerboard Motif

– an easy colorwork design for a beginner knitter that can be applied to any project

A
B

24 stitches

color block motifs

Worked over any number of stitches, using colors A and B

Knit all RS (odd-numbered) rows and purl all WS (even-numbered) rows, using the colors as indicated on the chart.

Reading from a chart Read knit (RS) rows from right to left and read purl (WS) rows from left to right.

When working large areas of color, use separate lengths or small balls of yarn for each area of color and twist the strands of yarn at the back of the work when changing colors to avoid a hole.

Spot Motif
– as an alternative, work each spot in a different color

A

B

pattern repeat = 24 stitches

Random Motif
- create and chart your own motifs

Worked over any number of stitches, using colors A and B

Knit all RS (odd-numbered) rows and purl all WS (even-numbered) rows, using the colors as indicated on the chart.

Reading from a chart Read knit (RS) rows from right to left and read purl (WS) rows from left to right.

When working large areas of color, use separate lengths or small balls of yarn for each area of color and twist the strands of yarn at the back of the work when changing colors to avoid a hole.

■ A
□ B

pattern repeat = 27 stitches

embellished motifs

Knitted fabric can be further embellished with embroidery, such as large areas of additional color, motifs, pattern detail, or vertical lines.

Worked over any number of stitches, using colors A, B, and C

Knit and purl alternate rows working the horizontal stripes using the color as indicated on the chart. When the knitting is complete, add the vertical stripes using duplicate stitch embroidery (see pages 34–35) in the color shown on the chart.

Plaid Motif
- any number of additional colors can be added in this way

A
B
C

29 stitches

Worked over any number of stitches

Knit and purl alternate rows working the larger areas of base color as indicated on the chart. When the knitting is complete, add the further detail colors using duplicate stitch embroidery (see pages 34–35) in the color shown on the chart.

Rose Motif
– use a needlepoint or embroidery design for inspiration

26 stitches

A
B
C
D
E
F
G

project
workshops

1 Faux Sheepskin Throw

Made in pure wool "fur" yarn, this sheepskin-shape throw is worked in simple garter stitch. It adds a striking and strong color statement to a chair, couch, or floor when two contrasting colors are "brought together" or juxtaposed.

Skill level...

BEGINNER

In this project you will learn...
Increasing and decreasing

Stitches used...
Garter stitch (knit every row)

Materials
4 x 100g hanks of super-bulky-weight "fur" yarn, such as Erika Knight *Fur Wool* (97% wool, 3% nylon binder; 44yd/40m per 3½oz/100g hank; (**6**) SUPER BULKY) in purple (Mulberry)
Pair of US size 17 (12mm) knitting needles
Large blunt-tipped sewing needle

Size
Approximately 36¾in (92cm) long and 21¾in (54.5cm) across widest point

Gauge
5½ sts and 11 rows to 4in (10cm) square measured over garter stitch using US size 17 (12mm) needles. Use smaller or larger needles if necessary to obtain the correct gauge.

Abbreviations
K2tog knit 2 sts together
See also page 143.

Note
Joining in a new ball
To achieve a neater finish, avoid joining in a new ball of yarn at the edge of your work.

3in (7cm)

11½in (29cm)

36¾in (92cm)

16in (40cm)

21¾in (54.5cm)

16in (40cm)

14½in (36.5cm)

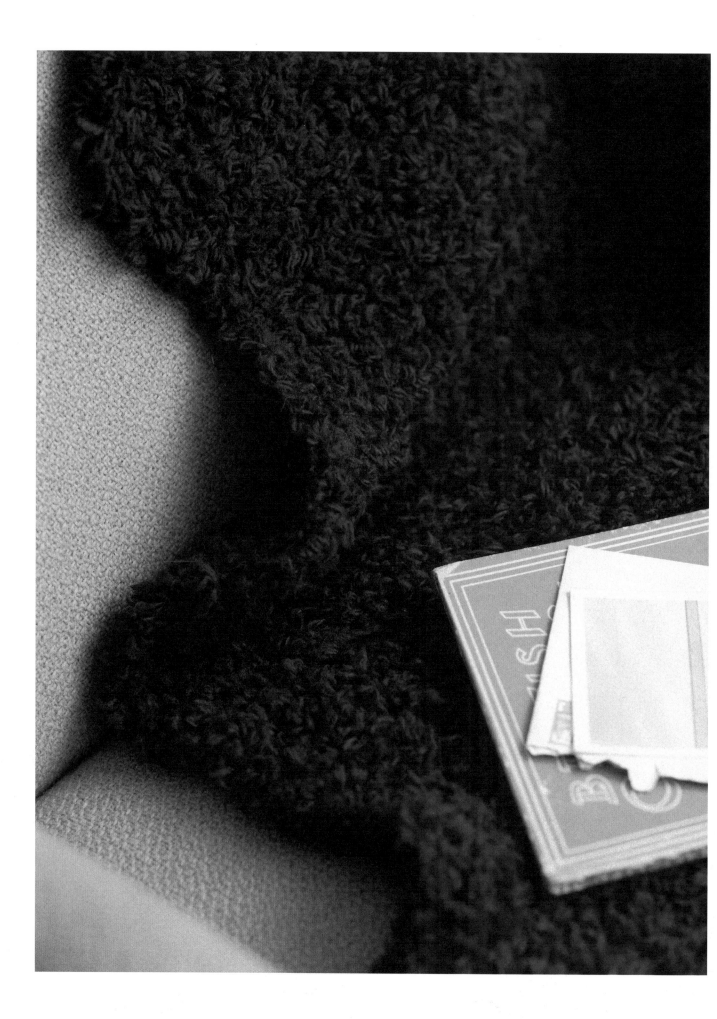

To make the throw

Cast on 20 sts and work in garter st (K every row) throughout as follows:

Row 1 K.
Row 2 Cast on 2 sts at beg of row, K to end. *22 sts.*
Row 3 Cast on 4 sts at beg of row, K to end. *26 sts.*
Row 4 Cast on 3 sts at beg of row, K to last 2 sts, K into front and back of next st, K1. *30 sts.*
Rows 5–13 K these 9 rows.
Row 14 K2tog, K to last 2 sts, K2tog. *28 sts.*
Rows 15–16 K these 2 rows.
Row 17 Rep row 14. *26 sts.*
Row 18 K.
Row 19 Rep row 14. *24 sts.*
Row 20 K.
Row 21 Rep row 14. *22 sts.*
Rows 22–25 K these 4 rows.
Row 26 K into front and back of first st, K to last 2 sts, K into front and back of next st, K1. *24 sts.*
Rows 27–28 K these 2 rows.
Row 29 Rep row 26. *26 sts.*
Rows 30–33 K these 4 rows.
Row 34 Rep row 26. *28 sts.*
Rows 35 K.
Row 36 Rep row 26. *30 sts.*
Rows 37–51 K these 15 rows.
Row 52 Rep row 14. *28 sts.*
Row 53 Rep row 14. *26 sts.*
Row 54 K.
Row 55 Rep row 14. *24 sts.*
Rows 56–58 K these 3 rows.
Row 59 Rep row 14. *22 sts.*
Rows 60–61 K these 2 rows.
Row 62 Rep row 26. *24 sts.*
Row 63 K.

Row 64 Rep row 26. *26 sts.*
Row 65 K.
Row 66 Rep row 26. *28 sts.*
Row 67 K.
Row 68 Rep row 26. *30 sts.*
Rows 69–71 K these 3 rows.
Row 72 Rep row 14. *28 sts.*
Rows 73–74 K these 2 rows.
Row 75 Bind off 2 sts at beg of row, K to end. *26 sts.*
Row 76 Bind off 2 sts at beg of row, K to end. *24 sts.*
Rows 77–78 K these 2 rows.
Row 79 Rep row 14. *22 sts.*
Rows 80–82 K these 3 rows.
Row 83 Rep row 14. *20 sts.*
Rows 84–85 K these 2 rows.
Row 86 Rep row 14. *18 sts.*
Rows 87–88 K these 2 rows.
Row 89 Rep row 14. *16 sts.*
Row 90 K.
Row 91 Rep row 14. *14 sts.*
Rows 92–93 K these 2 rows.
Row 94 Rep row 14. *12 sts.*
Rows 95–96 K these 2 rows.
Row 97 Rep row 14. *10 sts.*
Row 98 K.
Row 99 Bind off 2 sts at beg of row, K to last 2 sts, K2tog. *7 sts.*
Row 100 Bind off 2 sts at beg of row, K to end. *5 sts.*
Row 101 K2tog, K to end. *4 sts.*
Bind off.

To finish

Weave in any loose yarn ends.

2 Unisex Sweater

This basic raglan-sleeve sweater is knitted with a strand of two contrasting yarns "plied" together. It can be sewn together so either the smooth side or the reverse side of the stockinette stitch shows and is a great shared piece as the size range fits men and women.

Skill level

■■□□□
EASY

In this project you will learn...
Plying yarn

Stitches used

Stockinette stitch; K1, P1 rib; increasing and decreasing

Materials

Super-bulky-weight wool yarn, such as Erika Knight *Maxi Wool* (100% British wool; 87yd/80m per 3¹⁄₂oz/100g hank; (6) SUPER BULKY) in the following color:

    A off white (Canvas)—7(7:8:8:9:10) hanks

Aran-weight wool yarn, such as Erika Knight *Vintage Wool* (100% pure British wool; 95yd/87m per 1³⁄₄oz/50g hank; (4) MEDIUM) in the following color:

    B black (Pitch)—6(6:7:7:8:9) hanks

Size	XS	S	M	L	X	XXL
To fit chest (in)	34	36	38	40	42	44
To fit chest (cm)	86	91	97	102	107	112

Knitted measurements

Around chest (in)	39¹⁄₂	41¹⁄₂	43	45	47	49
Around chest (cm)	99	104	108	113	118	122
Length to shoulder (in)	25	26¹⁄₂	27¹⁄₄	28³⁄₄	29³⁄₄	31¹⁄₄
Length to shoulder (cm)	63.5	67	69	73	75	79
Sleeve seam (in)	18	18	18¹⁄₂	18¹⁄₂	19	19
Sleeve seam (cm)	46	46	47	47	48	48

Pair each of US sizes 15 and 17 (10mm and 12mm) knitting needles
US size 17 (12mm) circular knitting needle, for neckband
Large blunt-tipped sewing needle

Gauge

8¹⁄₂ sts and 11 rows to 4in (10cm) square measured over St st using US size 17 (12mm) needles and one strand of A and one strand of B held together. Use smaller or larger needles if necessary to obtain the correct gauge.

Abbreviations

See page 143.

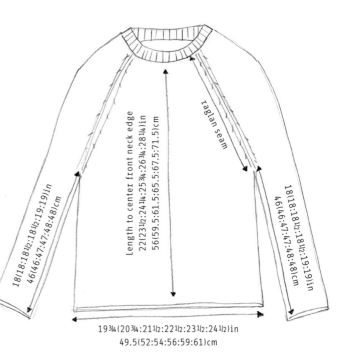

length to center front neck edge
22(23:23¹⁄₂:24¹⁄₄:25³⁄₄:26³⁄₄:28¹⁄₄)in
56(59.5:61.5:65.5:67.5:71.5)cm

raglan seam

18(18:18¹⁄₂:18¹⁄₂:19:19)in
46(46:47:47:48:48)cm

18(18:18¹⁄₂:18¹⁄₂:19:19)in
46(46:47:47:48:48)cm

19³⁄₄(20³⁄₄:21¹⁄₂:22¹⁄₂:23¹⁄₂:24¹⁄₂)in
49.5(52:54:56:59:61)cm

To make the sweater

Back

Using US size 15 (10mm) needles and one strand of A and one strand of B held tog, cast on 42(44:46:48:50:52) sts.

Beg with a K row, work 6 rows in St st.

Change to US size 17 (12mm) needles and cont in St st throughout, work until Back measures 15¾(16½:17¼:18:19:19¾)in/40(42:44:46:48:50)cm from cast-on edge, ending with RS facing for next row.

Shape raglan

Bind off 3 sts at beg of next 2 rows. *36(38:40:42:44:46) sts.*

Next row (dec on RS) K3, K2tog, K to last 5 sts, K2tog tbl, K3. *34(36:38:40:42:44) sts.*

Next row P.

Next row Dec 1 st at both ends of row as set. *32(34:36:38:40:42) sts.*

Next row (dec on WS) P3, P2tog tbl, P to last 5 sts, P2tog, P3. *30(32:34:36:38:40) sts.*

Working decs as set, dec 1 st at both ends of next row and every foll alt row until 12(12:14: 14:16:16) sts rem, then on foll row, so ending with RS facing for bind-off.

Bind off rem 10(10:12:12:14:14) sts.

Front

Work as given for Back until 20(20:20:22:22:22) sts rem, so ending with WS facing for next row.

P 1 row.

Shape neck

Next row (RS) K3, K2tog, K2tog tbl, K1, turn leaving rem sts unworked.

Next row P1, P2tog, P3.

Next row K1, sl 1, K2tog, psso, K1.

Next row P3tog and fasten off.

With RS facing, slip center 4(4:4:6:6:6) sts onto a st holder, rejoin yarn, and work as follows:

Next row K1, K2tog, K2tog tbl, K3.

Next row P3, P2tog tbl, P1.

Next row K1, K3tog tbl, K1.

Next row P3tog and fasten off.

Sleeves

Using US size 15 (10mm) needles and one strand of A and one strand of B held tog, cast on 24(26:28:28:30:32) sts.

Beg with a K row, work 6 rows in St st.

Change to US size 17 (12mm) needles and work as follows:

Next row (inc) K3, M1, K to last 3 sts, M1, K3.

Cont in St st throughout, inc 1 st at both ends of every foll 10th row until there are 34(36:38:38:40:42) sts.

Cont without shaping until work measures 18(18:18½:18½:19:19)in/46(46:47:47:48:48)cm from cast-on edge, ending with RS facing for next row.

Shape raglan

Bind off 3 sts at beg of next 2 rows. *28(30:32:32:34:36) sts.*

Next row (dec on RS) K3, K2tog, K to last 5 sts, K2tog tbl, K3.

Work 3 rows without shaping, so ending with RS facing for next row.

Working decs as set, dec 1 st at both ends of next row and every foll alt row until 12 sts rem, so ending with WS facing for next row.

P 1 row.

For left sleeve only

Dec 1 st at both ends of next row. *10 sts.*

Bind off 3 sts at beg of next row. *7 sts.*

Dec 1 st at beg of next row. *6 sts.*

Bind off 3 sts at beg of next row. *3 sts.*

Bind off rem 3 sts.

For right sleeve only

Bind off 4 sts at beg and dec 1 st at end of next row. *7 sts.*

P 1 row.

Bind off 3 sts at beg and dec 1 st at end of next row. *3 sts.*

P 1 row.

Bind off rem 3 sts.

Neckband

Gently steam the pieces on the reverse, but allow bottom edges of Sleeves, Back, and Front to curl up onto the right side of the garment.

Sew together both front and back raglan seams. With RS facing and using US size 17 (12mm) circular needle and one strand of A and one strand of B held tog, pick up and K 10(10:12: 12:14:14) sts across back neck, 10 sts across left sleeve, 4 sts down right neck, K 4(4:4:6:6:6) sts from holder at front neck, pick up and K 4 sts up right neck and 10 sts across right sleeve. *42(42:44:46:48:48) sts.*

Work 3 rounds in K1, P1 rib.

Bind off in rib.

To finish

Weave in any loose yarn ends.

Sew together side and sleeve seams.

3 Phased Throw

The dip-dyed or phased color effect in this simple garter-stitch throw is created by using two balls of tonal hand-dyed yarn held together as one yarn, to create beautiful subtle shades. The throw is finished at one end with a binding of soft leather.

Skill level

■□□□
BEGINNER

In this project you will learn…
Plying; phasing colors

Stitches used
Garter stitch (K every row)

Materials
Double-knitting-weight hand-dyed wool yarn,
  such as Madeline Tosh *Tosh DK* (100% superwash
  merino wool; 225yd/206m per 3½oz/100g hank;
  (3) LIGHT) in the following 5 colors:
  A brown (Twig)—2 hanks
  B bright aqua blue (Baltic)—2 hanks
  C dark denim blue (Worn Denim)—2 hanks
  D gray aqua (Cove)—2 hanks
  E light green-blue (Well Water)—2 hanks
US size 15 (10mm) circular knitting needle, 40in
  (100cm) long
Piece of fine soft brown leather, for binding one
  end of throw

*Note: Yarn amounts given are based on average
requirements and are approximate.*

Size
Approximately 48¾in x 56½in (122cm x 141.5cm)

Gauge
10 sts and 14 rows to 4in (10cm) square measured over garter stitch using US size 15 (10mm) needles and two strands of yarn held together. Use larger or smaller needles if necessary to obtain the correct gauge.

Abbreviations
See page 143.

Notes
Knitting in rows with a long circular needle
The throw is knitted back and forth in rows on the long circular needle to accommodate the large number of stitches.

Joining in a new color for stripes
On the row before you need the new color, work to the last stitch. Taking the end of the new color, use together with the yarn in work to work the last stitch, creating a "double stitch." On the first stitch of next row, work the double stitch as one stitch with just the end of the new color. This will securely "anchor" your new yarn and neither create unsightly knots nor create bumps.

Preparing the yarn
Wind the hanks of hand-dyed yarn into balls and label each color A, B, C, D, and E.

E + E

D + E

D + D

C + D

C + C

B + C

B+ B

A + B

A + A

56½in (141.5cm)

48¾in (122cm)

A

B

C

D

E

To make the throw

Using two strands of A held together as one yarn (A+A), cast on 122 sts.

Working in garter st (K every row) throughout, work in bands of phased color as follows:

Band 1
Cont to use A+A, work 22 rows, approximately 6in (15cm).

Band 2
Drop one strand of A and introduce one strand of B (A+B), then work 22 rows, approximately 6in (15cm).

Band 3
Drop A and introduce another strand of B (B+B), then work 22 rows, approximately 6in (15cm).

Band 4
Drop one strand of B and introduce one strand of C (B+C), then work 22 rows, approximately 6in (15cm).

Band 5
Drop B and introduce another strand of C (C+C), then work 22 rows, approximately 6in (15cm).

Band 6
Drop one strand of C and introduce an one strand of D (C+D), then work 22 rows, approximately 6in (15cm).

Band 7
Drop C and introduce another strand of D (D+D), then work 22 rows, approximately 6in (15cm).

Band 8
Drop one strand of D and introduce one strand of E (D+E), then work 22 rows, approximately 6in (15cm).

Band 9
Drop D and introduce another strand of E (E+E), then work 22 rows, approximately 6in (15cm).
Bind off.

To finish

Weave in any loose yarn ends.
Cut the brown leather into narrow strips ½in (12mm) wide. Use the strips to bind the cast-on edge with overcast stitches, knotting in a new strip when necessary and leaving loose ends.

4 Primary Striped Throw

A colorful, vibrant, and easy to knit "wrap-a-round" throw is created here using a simple technique to join in new colors. It is knitted in super-bulky wool yarn and has wide crisp rib borders at the top and bottom and neat narrow rib selvage edges.

Skill level

EASY

In this project you will learn...
Joining in new colors

Stitches used
Stockinette stitch; K2, P2 rib

Materials
Super-bulky-weight wool yarn, such as Erika Knight *Maxi Wool* (100% British wool; 87yd/80m per 3½oz/100g hank; SUPER BULKY) in the following 6 colors:

    A dark dusky green (Gunk 021)—3 hanks
    B black (Pitch 025)—2 hanks
    C off white (Canvas 001)—1 hank
    D brown (Milk Chocolate 044)—3 hanks
    E tomato red (Manga 047)—1 hank
    F olive green (Artisan 020)—2 hanks

US size 17 (12mm) circular knitting needle, 40in (100cm) long
Large blunt-tipped sewing needle

Size
Approximately 46in x 59½in (115cm x 149cm)

Gauge
8½ sts and 12 rows to 4in (10cm) square measured over St st using US size 17 (12mm) needles. Use smaller or larger needles if necessary to obtain the correct gauge.

Abbreviations
See page 143.

Notes
Knitting in rows with a long circular needle
The throw is knitted back and forth in rows on the long circular needle to accommodate the large number of stitches.

Joining in a new ball
Ensure that you have sufficient yarn to complete a row to avoid joining in a new ball in the middle of a row.

Joining in a new color for stripes
On the row before you need the new color, work to the last stitch. Taking the end of the new color, use together with the yarn in work to work the last stitch, creating a "double stitch." On the first stitch of next row, work the double stitch as one stitch with just the end of the new color. This will securely "anchor" your new yarn and neither create unsightly knots nor create bumps.

Stripe sequence

A 14 rows (in rib)
B 32 rows
C 7 rows
D 44 rows
C 4 rows
B 9 rows
C 3 rows
E 12 rows
C 3 rows
F 19 rows
C 5 rows
A 14 rows
A 14 rows (in rib)

56½in (144cm)

46in (115cm)

Using A, cast on 98 sts.
Work in rib as follows:
Row 1 (RS) [K2, P2] to last 2 sts, K2.
Row 2 P2, [K2, P2] to end of row.
Rep the last 2 rows 6 times more—this completes
the first 14 rows worked in A (as indicated in
Stripe Sequence left).
Change to B and cont in St st with rib selvage
edges as follows:
Next row (RS) K2, P2, K to last 4 sts, P2, K2.
Next row P2, K2, P to last 4 sts, K2, P2.
Rep the last 2 rows until the 32-row stripe in B
has been completed.
Change to C and cont in St st with rib selvage
edges as set **and at the same time** follow the
Stripe Sequence starting with the 7-row stripe in
C until the last 14-row St st stripe in A has been
completed, so ending with RS facing for next row.
Then still using A, work in rib as follows:
Row 1 (RS) (K2, P2) to last 2 sts, K2.
Row 2 P2, (K2, P2) to end of row.
Rep the last 2 rows 6 times more—this completes
the last 14 rows worked in A.
Bind off in rib.

To finish

Weave in any loose yarn ends.
Lay the work out flat and gently steam on the
reverse to enhance the yarn, avoiding the
ribbing.

Stripe and Print Pillow

An easy way to ensure colors work together is to take the palette from a painting, textile, or ceramic. The vibrant colors of a Liberty print fabric form the basis of this contemporary pillow. The mercerized cotton yarn gives a fresh appearance and works well with the fabric back.

Skill level

EASY

In this project you will learn...
How to change colors

Stitches used...
Stockinette stitch

Materials
Fine-weight cotton yarn, such as Rowan *Cotton Glacé* (100% mercerized cotton; 125yd/115m per 1¾oz/50g ball; **2** FINE) in the following 8 colors:
   A light gray (Dawn Grey 831)—1 ball
   B plum (Garnet 841)—1 ball
   C mustard (Dijon 739)—1 ball
   D turquoise (Winsor 849)—1 ball
   E dark red (blood orange 445)—1 ball
   F bright pink (Bubbles 724)—1 ball
   G black (Black 727)—1 ball
   H **pale** green (Shoot 814)—1 ball
Pair of US size 5 (3.75mm) knitting needles
Large blunt-tipped sewing needle
1½yd (50cm) of a cotton fabric print, for back
Sewing needle and matching sewing thread, for fabric back
Rectangular feather pillow form, 15in x 12in (38cm x 30cm)

Note: Yarn amounts given are based on average requirements and are approximate.

Size
Approximately 15in x 12in (38cm x 30cm)

Gauge
22 sts and 32 rows to 4in (10cm) square measured over St st using 3.75mm (US 5) needles. Use larger or smaller needles if necessary to obtain the correct gauge.

Abbreviations
See page 143.

Note
Joining in a new color for stripes
On the row before you need the new color, work to the last stitch. Taking the end of the new color, use together with the yarn in work to work the last stitch, creating a "double stitch." On the first stitch of next row, work the double stitch as one stitch with just the end of the new color. This will securely "anchor" your new yarn and neither create unsightly knots nor create bumps.

To make the pillow-cover front
Using A, cast on 66 sts.
Beg with a K row, work in St st in the following
stripe sequence:
A 3 rows
B 5 rows
C 5 rows
D 3 rows
E 5 rows
C 5 rows
A 3 rows
F 7 rows
A 1 row
G 2 rows
A 5 rows
E 3 rows
H 7 rows
G 6 rows
A 3 rows
B 2 rows
C 3 rows
B 4 rows
E 4 rows
F 6 rows
A 3 rows
D 5 rows
C 3 rows

F 2 rows
A 4 rows
G 3 rows
H 4 rows
D 3 rows
B 5 rows
D 1 row
E 4 rows
A 3 rows
Bind off.

To finish the pillow-cover front
Weave in any loose yarn ends.
Lay the work out flat and gently steam on the
reverse to enhance the yarn.

To add the fabric pillow-cover back
Cut a piece of fabric the same size as the knitted
front plus 1⁄2in (1.5cm) extra all around for the
seam allowance.
With right sides together, pin the pillow-cover
front to the fabric along the seam lines, easing to
fit. Using matching thread and a sewing needle,
stitch the knitted front to the fabric back piece
around three sides.
Turn the pillow cover right side out. Insert the
pillow form and sew the remaining side closed.

6 Diagonal Stripe Dishcloths

Take color inspiration from the simplest of sources, for example, the crisp white and bold stripe linens of utilitarian dish towels. With its narrow stripes, this traditional "diagonal" square is knitted in garter stitch in hemp yarn, which is sustainable and naturally abrasive.

Skill level

EASY

In this project you will learn...
Joining in a new color; using the wrong side of the stripe; increasing and decreasing

Stitches used
Garter stitch (K every row)

Materials
Double-knitting-weight hemp yarn, such as
  Lana Knits *Allhemp6* (100% hemp; 165yd/150m
  per 3½oz/100g hank; (**3**) LIGHT) in the following
  3 colors:
    A off white (Pearl 010)—1 hank
    B red (Raspberry 011)—1 hank
    C beige (Classic 012)—1 hank
Pair of US size 5 (3.75mm) knitting needles
Large blunt-tipped sewing needle

Size
Approximately 10in x 10in (25cm x 25cm)

Gauge
17 sts and 37 rows to 4in (10cm) square measured over garter stitch using US size 5 (3.75mm) needles. Use smaller or larger needles if necessary to obtain the correct gauge.

Abbreviations
K2tog knit 2 sts together
See also page 143.

Note
Joining in a new color for stripes
On the row before you need the new color, work to the last stitch. Taking the end of the new color, use together with the yarn in work to work the last stitch, creating a "double stitch". On the first stitch of next row, work the double stitch as one stitch with just the end of the new color. This will securely "anchor" your new yarn and neither create unsightly knots nor create bumps.

To make the white dishcloth with red stripes
Using A, cast on 2 sts.
Row 1 K1, K into front and back of last st (to inc 1 st). *3 sts.*
Row 2 K2, K into front and back of last st. *4 sts.*
Row 3 K to last st, K into front and back of last st. *5 sts.*
Rep row 3 until there are 62 sts on needle.
Next row K.
Next row (dec) K to last 2 sts, K2tog (to dec 1 st). *61 sts.*
Rep last row until 43 sts rem.
Cont to dec as set **and at the same time** work stripes as follows:
B 2 rows
A 3 rows
B 4 rows
A 3 rows
B 2 rows
Using A, cont to dec as set until 2 sts rem.
Next row K2tog and fasten off.

To make the white dishcloth with beige and red stripes
Using A, cast on 2 sts.
Row 1 K1, K into front and back of last st (to inc 1 st). *3 sts.*
Row 2 K2, K into front and back of last st. *4 sts.*
Row 3 K to last st, K into front and back of last st. *5 sts.*
Rep row 3 until there are 19 sts on needle.
Cont to inc as set, work 4 rows in C.
Using A, cont to inc as set until there are 62 sts on needle.
Next row K.
Next row (dec) K to last 2 sets, K2tog (to dec 1 st). *61 sts.*
Rep last row until 53 sts rem.
Cont to dec as set **and at the same time** work stripes as follows:
C 4 rows
A 2 rows
B 2 rows
A 2 rows
B 2 rows
A 2 rows
C 4 rows
Using A, cont to dec as set until 2 sts rem.
Next row K2tog and fasten off.

To finish both dishcloths
Weave in any loose yarn ends.
Lay the work out flat and gently steam on the reverse to enhance the yarn.

7 Patterned Pouffe

Here's a quick and fun lesson in striping, to make a practical pouffe. Rib stitch stripes create an energetic "broken" pattern and a vibrant textile, which is perfect for this colorful pouffe where a tight fit over the inner beanbag is required.

Skill level

EASY

In this project you will learn...
How to change color; working even- and odd-row stripes

Stitches used
K1, P1 rib; K1, P2 rib

Materials
Super-bulky-weight wool yarn, such as Erika
  Knight *Maxi Wool* (100% British wool; 87yd/80m
  per 3½oz/100g hank; **(6)** SUPER BULKY) in the
  following 8 colors:
    A pale gray (Flax 002)—2 hanks
    B black (Pitch 025)—1 hanks
    C aqua blue (Mallard 031)—1 hank
    D burgundy red (House Red 046)—1 hank
    E light blue (Steve 032)—1 hank
    F medium gray (Storm 004)—1 hank
    G steel blue (Classic 038)—1 hank
    H bright red (Marni 030)—1 hank
US size 13 (9mm) circular knitting needle, 40in
  (100cm) long
Inexpensive beanbag (or duvet or polystyrene
  beads in a fabric bag)

*Note: Yarn amounts given are based on average
requirements and are approximate.*

Size
Finished pouffe is approximately 15½in (39cm)
high and 65in (165cm) in circumference

Gauge
10 sts and 14 rows to 4in (10cm) square measured
over rib patt using US size 13 (9mm) needles. Use
smaller or larger needles if necessary to obtain
the correct gauge.

Abbreviations
K3tog tbl knit 3 sts together through back loops
P2tog purl 2 sts together
See also page 143.

Notes
Knitting in rows with a long circular needle
The pouffe cover is knitted back and forth in
rows on the long circular needle to accommodate
the large number of stitches.

Joining in a new color for stripes
On the row before you need the new color, work
to the last stitch. Taking the end of the new color,
use together with the yarn in work to work the
last stitch, creating a "double stitch." On the first
stitch of next row, work the double stitch as one
stitch with just the end of the new color. This
will securely "anchor" your new yarn and neither
create unsightly knots nor create bumps.

Stripe sequence

*B 5 rows
C 1 row
A 2 rows
B 1 row
D 4 rows on first rep; H 4 rows on second rep
E 1 row
F 3 rows
B 2 rows
C 6 rows
B 1 row
E 1 row
G 1 row
E 1 row
A 1 row
F 1 row
A 1 row
C 1 row
A 4 rows
D 1 row on first rep; H 1 row on second rep
A 2 rows
F 1 row
G 8 rows
A 1 row
Repeat sequence starting from *.

To make the pouffe cover
Using B, cast on 34 sts.
Row 1 K.
Row 2 [K into front and back in each st] to last st, K1. *67 sts.*
Row 3 K.
Row 4 [K into front and back in each st] to end of row. *134 sts.*
Keeping Stripe Sequence correct (see left), cont in rib as follows:
Row 1 (RS) Using B, [P2, K1] to last 2 sts, P2.
Row 2 Using C, [K2, P1] to last 2 sts, K2.
Starting with first 2-row stripe in A, cont in Stripe Sequence throughout **and at the same time** rep last 2 rows until 88 rows have been worked from cast-on edge and work measures approximately 25in (63cm), ending with RS facing for next row.
Keeping Stripe Sequence correct dec as follows:
Row 1 (RS) [P2tog, K1] to last 2 sts, P2tog. *89 sts.*
Row 2 [K1, P1] to last st, K1.
Row 3 [P1, K3tog tbl) to last st, P1. *45 sts.*
Row 4 [K1, P1] to last st, K1.
Row 5 [P1, K3tog tbl] to last st, P1. *23 sts.*
Cut yarn, leaving a long end.
Thread yarn end through rem sts, pull up tightly, and fasten securely. Don't cut the yarn but use it to sew side seam, stopping about 12in (30cm) from the cast-on edge.

To finish
Insert the beanbag inners.
Finish sewing side seam and fasten securely.
Thread yarn through the cast-on edge, pull up tightly, and fasten securely.

Boot
Toppers

This slip-stitch color pattern creates a great textile on each side, so it's a difficult choice which to use. It has quite a retro "Fair Isle" appearance so is certain to be a firm favorite. These simple boot toppers are a great project to try in this stitch.

Skill level

EASY

In this project you will learn...
How to work a slip-stitch color pattern

Stitches used
Stockinette stitch slip-stitch color pattern; K1, P1 rib

Materials
Aran-weight wool yarn, such as Erika Knight *Vintage Wool* (100% pure British wool; 95yd/87m per 1¾oz/50g hank; (4) MEDIUM) in the following 7 colors:
   A light gray (Drizzle)—1 hank
   B dark grape (Mulberry)—1 hank
   C light blue (Steve)—1 hank
   D dark blue (Dark)—1 hank
   E fuchsia (Gorgeous)—1 hank
   F light brown (Bambi)—1 hank
   G pale beige (Flax)—1 hank
Pair of US size 8 (5mm) knitting needles
Large blunt-tipped sewing needle

Note: Yarn amounts given are based on average requirements and are approximate.

Size
One size
Approximately 14¼in (36cm) in circumference around slip-stitch pattern, unstretched

Gauge
18 sts and 24 rows to 4in (10cm) square measured over St st using US size 8 (5mm) needles. Use larger or smaller needles if necessary to obtain the correct gauge.

Abbreviations
See page 143.

Note
Working the slip-stitch color pattern
Only one color is used in each row of the slip-stitch color pattern. When slipping stitches on right-side rows hold the yarn at the back of the work and when slipping stitches on a wrong-side row hold the yarn at the front of the work. All slip stitches are slipped purlwise, inserting the needle into the stitches you are slipping as if to purl (see page 36).

To make the boot toppers
Using A, cast on 74 sts.
Row 1 (RS) Using A, K.
Row 2 Using A, P.
Row 3 Using B, K2, *sl 4, K2; rep from * to end.
Row 4 Using B, P3, sl 2, *P4, sl 2; rep from * to last 3 sts, P3.
Rows 5 Using B, K.
Row 6 Using B, P.
Row 7 Using C, K1, sl 2, K2, *sl 4, K2; rep from * to last 3 sts, sl 2, K1.
Row 8 Using C, P1, sl 1, P4, *sl 2, P4; rep from * to last 2 sts, sl 1, P1.
Rows 9 Using C, K.
Row 10 Using C, P.
Rows 11 Using D, K2, *sl 4, K2; rep from * to end.
Row 12 Using D, P3, sl 2, *P4, sl 2; rep from * to last 3 sts, P3.
Rows 13 Using D, K.
Row 14 Using D, P.
Rows 15 Using E, K1, sl 2, K2, *sl 4, K2; rep from * to last 3 sts, sl 2, K1.
Row 16 Using E, P1, sl 1, P4, *sl 2, P4; rep from * to last 2 sts, sl 1, P1.
Row 17 Using E, K.
Row 18 Using E, P.
Row 19 Using B, K2, *sl 4, K2; rep from * to end.
Row 20 Using B, P3, sl 2, *P4, sl 2; rep from * to last 3 sts, P3.
Row 21 Using B, K.
Row 22 Using B, P.
Row 23 Using F, K1, sl 2, K2, *sl 4, K2; rep from * to last 3 sts, sl 2, K1.
Row 24 Using F, P1, sl 1, P4, *sl 2, P4; rep from * to last 2 sts, sl 1, P1.
Row 25 Using F, K.

Row 26 Using F, P.
Row 27 Using G, K2, *sl 4, K2; rep from * to end.
Row 28 Using G, P3, sl 2, *P4, sl 2; rep from * to last 3 sts, P3.
Row 29 Using G, K.
Row 30 Using G, P.
Row 31 Using D, K1, sl 2, K2, *sl 4, K2; rep from * to last 3 sts, sl 2, K1.
Row 32 Using D, P1, sl 1, P4, *sl 2, P4; rep from * to last 2 sts, sl 1, P1.

Cont in K1, P1 rib as follows:
D 2 rows
B 1 row
A 4 rows
E 1 row
D 3 rows
B 2 rows
C 6 rows
B 1 row
E 1 row
F 1 row
E 1 row
G 1 row
D 1 row
G 1 row
C 1 row
G 2 rows
Bind off in rib.

To finish
Weave in any loose yarn ends.
Lay the work out flat and gently steam on the reverse to enhance the yarn, avoiding the ribbing.
Sew the side seam.

Tweed Stitch Muffler Scarf

The colors of men's silk foulard patterns and quintessential British tweeds are the inspiration for this simple "tweed" stitch muffler. Worked in three colors in soft linen for drape, stitch clarity, and richness of tones, it also has a contrasting teal bound-off edge.

Skill level...

EASY

In this project you will learn...
How to work a slip-stitch color pattern

Stitches used...
Slip-stitch color pattern

Materials
Double-knitting-weight linen-cotton yarn, such as
  Rowan *Creative Linen* (50% linen, 50% cotton;
  219yd/200m per 3½oz/100g hank; **(3)** LIGHT)
  in the following 4 colors:
    A dark steel blue (Stormy 635)—1 hank
    B maroon red (Coleus 637)—1 hank
    C light green (Apple 629)—1 hank
    D light teal blue (Teal 625)—1 hank
Pair of US size 8 (5mm) knitting needles
Large blunt-tipped sewing needle

Size
Approximately 7in x 40½in (17.5cm x 102cm)

Gauge
26 sts and 34 rows to 4in (10cm) square measured over pattern using US size 8 (5mm) needles. Use larger or smaller needles if necessary to obtain the correct gauge.

Abbreviations
See page 143.

Note
Working the slip-stitch color pattern
Only one color is used in each row of the slip-stitch pattern. All slip stitches are slipped purlwise, inserting the needle into the stitches you are slipping as if to purl (see page 36).

To make the scarf
Using A, cast on 45 sts.
Set-up row (WS) Using A, P.
Row 1 (RS) Using B, K1, *yf, sl 1, yb, K1; rep from * to end.
Row 2 Using C, K1, P1, * yb, sl 1, yf, P1; rep from * to last st, K1.
Row 3 Using A, rep row 1.
Row 4 Using B, rep row 2.
Row 5 Using C, rep row 1.
Row 6 Using A, rep row 2.
Rep last 6 rows until work measures 39½in (100cm) from cast-on edge, ending with RS facing for next row.
Change to D and work 4 rows in patt.
Bind off in patt using D.

To finish
Weave in any loose yarn ends.
Lay the work out flat and gently steam on the reverse to enhance the yarn.

Fair Isle Snood

The "stranding" on the inside of the knitting on this simple Fair Isle pattern in classic black and white creates a "woven fabric" effect—always a favorite of mine when allowed to show. The cast-on and bind-off rows are each worked in a contrasting color to accentuate this effect.

Skill level

EXPERIENCED

In this project you will learn...
Working in the round; working with two colors in a round using the stranding technique

Stitches used
Knit

Materials
Aran-weight wool yarn, such as Erika Knight *Vintage Wool* (100% pure British wool; 95yd/87m per 1¾oz/50g hank; **4** MEDIUM) in the following 4 colors:
- **A** pale beige (Flax)—3 hanks
- **B** black (Pitch)—2 hanks
- **C** fuchsia (Gorgeous)—small amount
- **D** aqua (Leighton)—small amount

US size 8 (5mm) circular knitting needle, 30in (75cm) long
Large blunt-tipped sewing needle

Size
Approximately 40in x 12¾in (100cm x 32cm)

Gauge
18 sts and 21 rows to 4in (10cm) square measured over Fair Isle pattern using US size 8 (5mm) needles. Use larger or smaller needles if necessary to obtain the correct gauge.

Abbreviations
See page 143.

Notes

Working the pattern in rounds from the chart
When working the stockinette stitch Fair Isle pattern in rounds on the circular needle note that every stitch is a knit stitch, and read all rows of the chart from right to left.

Stranding
Work the Fair Isle pattern using the stranding technique. No more that two colors are used in a row, and the color not in use is stranded at the back of the knitting (see pages 28–31).

To make the snood
Using US size 8 (5mm) circular needle and C, cast on 180 sts.
Place a st marker on tip of right needle to mark start of round, then K 1 round.
Change to yarn A and using the stranding technique, work chart rounds 2–66 in St st (knit every round), changing color where indicated, reading all rows from right to left, and working the 36-st chart repeat 5 times for each round.
Using D, K 1 round (chart round 67).
Bind off in D.

To finish
Weave in any loose yarn ends.
Lay the work out flat and gently steam on the reverse to enhance the yarn.

	A
	B
	C
	D

patt repeat = 36 sts (entire width of chart)

Houndstooth Hat

This basic beanie-shaped hat has a rolled edge at the brim. It is knitted in a two-color houndstooth pattern using the simple "stranding" technique and is topped off with a huge impressive two-color pompom.

Skill level

EXPERIENCED

In this project you will learn...
How to knit a pattern with two colors in a row using the stranding technique; how to make a pompom

Stitches used
Stockinette stitch

Materials
Super-bulky-weight wool yarn, such as Erika Knight *Maxi Wool* (100% British wool; 87yd/80m per 3½oz/100g hank; 6 SUPER BULKY) in the following 2 colors:
For the green and black version
   A olive green (Artisan 020)—1 hank
   B black (Pitch 025)—1 hank
For the tomato red and black version
   A tomato red (Manga 214)—1 hank
   B black (Pitch 025)—1 hank
Pair of US size 17 (12mm) knitting needles
Large blunt-tipped sewing needle
Piece of stiff cardboard, for making pompom

Note: Yarn amounts given are based on average requirements and are approximate.

Size
One size to fit average adult head
Approximately 20½in (51cm) in circumference, unstretched

Gauge
10 sts and 10½ rows measured over 4in (10cm) square over color pattern with US size 17 (12mm) needles. Use larger or smaller needles if necessary to obtain the correct gauge.

Abbreviations
K2tog knit 2 sts together
See also page 143.

Notes
Working the pattern from the chart
When working the stockinette stitch houndstooth pattern in rows, read all knit (odd-numbered) rows from right to left and all purl (even-numbered) rows from left to right.

Stranding
Work the houndstooth pattern using the stranding technique. Two colors are used in a row, and the color not in use is stranded at the back of the knitting (see pages 28–31).

To make the hat

Using B, cast on 51 sts.

Beg with a K row, work in St st houndstooth pattern from chart using the stranding technique as follows:

Row 1 (RS) Following 10-st chart pattern repeat from right to left, work [K1B, K7A, K2B] 5 times, then work first st of pattern repeat once more (that is, K1B).

Row 2 Work last st (at right of chart) of pattern repeat (that is, P1B), then following 10-st chart pattern repeat from left to right, work [P1B, P8A, P1B] 5 times.

These 2 rows set chart placement.

Cont in patt, working 14-row repeat as set on chart once, then rows 1–10 once more, so ending with RS facing for next row.

Using A only, cont as follows:

Next row [Sl 1, K2tog, psso] 17 times. *17 sts.*

Cut yarn leaving a long end, thread end through remaining sts, pull up tightly, and fasten securely.

To finish

Sew the hat seam.

Weave in any loose yarns ends.

Gently steam the work on the reverse to enhance the yarn.

To make the pompom

Cut out two cardboard circles approximately 5in (13cm) in diameter and cut an identical 1in (2.5cm) hole in the center of each one.

Hold the circles together and using B wound into a ball small enough to pass through the center of the hole, wind the yarn over the circles, keeping the strands close together. Add a layer of A in the same way. Alternating B and A, work as many layers as you can before the center of the hole becomes too small for a ball to pass through.

Using sharp scissors, slip one of the blades between the two layers of cardboard and cut around the circle and through the yarn.

Wrap a length of yarn tightly around the center off the pompom between the two cardboard circles and knot the yarn securely, leaving long ends to secure the pompom to the hat. Cut away the cardboard.

Then shake, fluff and trim the pompom and sew it to the top of the hat.

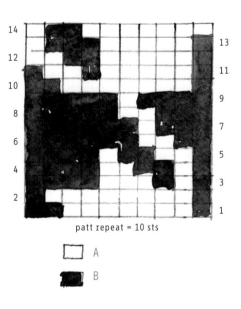

patt repeat = 10 sts

☐ A

■ B

12 Scandi Socks

These Fair Isle pattern slouchy socks are worked with five double-pointed needles. The pattern is knitted using the stranding technique and looks great in two or even three colors. Alternatively work each pattern section in different colors for a really personal effect.

Skill level

EXPERIENCED

In this project you will learn...
Working in the round; working with two colors in a round using the stranding technique (see pages 28–30)

Stitches used
Knit

Materials
Double-knitting-weight wool yarn, such as Erika Knight *British Blue Wool* (100% Blue-Faced Leicester wool; 60yd/55m per ¾oz/25g ball; **3** LIGHT) in the following 2 colors:
    A gray (Mouse 039)—3 balls
    B pale gold (Gift 040)—3 balls
Set of five US size 5 (3.75mm) double-pointed knitting needles
Set of five US size 6 (4mm) double-pointed knitting needles
Large blunt-tipped sewing needle

Note: Yarn amounts given are based on average requirements and are approximate.

Size
To fit an average woman's foot, length 8–10in (20–25cm)
Knitted measurements (unstretched)
Foot circumference 8in (20cm)
Leg circumference 10in (25cm)
Length from sole 12in (30cm)

Gauge
24 sts and 27 rows to 4in (10cm) square measured over color pattern using US size 6 (4mm) needles. Use larger or smaller needles if necessary to obtain the correct gauge.

Abbreviations
See page 143.

patt repeat = 12 sts

□ A
□ B

To make the left sock

Using US size 5 (3.75mm) double-pointed needles and B, cast on 60 sts, distributing them evenly over four needles.

Place a marker to mark beg of round and join to work in the round, taking care not to twist sts and using fifth needle to knit with.

K 18 rounds, ending at marker.

Change to A and K 12 rounds, ending at marker.

Fold up hem

Next round K the first st of round tog with corresponding loop from cast-on edge, then rep this process with each st and its corresponding cast-on loop to end of round.

Change to US size 6 (4mm) needles and using A, K 2 rounds.

Begin chart

[Knitting every round, work chart rounds 1–20] twice, repeating 12-st patt repeat 5 times in each round and using the stranding technique.

Rep chart rounds 1–6 once more.

Cont in A only, K 2 rounds.

Next round *K3, K2tog; rep from * to end. *48 sts.*

K 2 rounds.**

Place sts for heel

Cut yarn and slip first 24 sts purlwise without working them.

With a strand of contrasting waste yarn about 24in (60cm) long, K 24 sts and slip next 24 sts.

Rejoin A and K the 24 sts worked in waste yarn, then K to end of round.

Place marker to mark beg of round.

Using A, K 3 rounds, making first and last sts slightly tighter to prevent holes.

Begin chart

Work chart rounds 1–20, repeating 12-st patt repeat 4 times in each round; then rep chart rounds 1–7 once more.

Using A, K 2 rounds.

Work toe

Change to 3.75mm (US size 3) needles and B.

Decrease round 1 *K1, K2tog tbl, K18, K2tog, K1*, place marker; rep from * to * once more.

Note: The two markers mark the positions of the decreases.

K 2 rounds without shaping.

Decrease round 2 *K1, K2tog tbl, K to 3 sts before marker, K2tog, K1*; rep from * to * once more.

K 1 round without shaping.

Rep last 2 rounds twice more.

Cont to work *decrease round 2* on every foll round until 8 sts rem.

K2, and split the sts over 2 needles from back to front, so there are now 2 sts from the instep and 2 sts from the sole on each of the two needles.

Cut yarn, leaving a 5in (13cm) tail, and graft sts together using Kitchener stitch.

Work heel

Remove waste yarn at heel and pick up the live sts on each side of the opening. Using US size 6 (4mm) double-pointed needles, distribute the sts evenly over the needles, so the 24 sts for the top of the heel are on two needles and the bottom 24 sts are on the other two needles. Place markers at each side of the heel opening where you will be making the decreases.

Note: Sometimes it helps to pick up an extra 2 sts either side of each marker to reduce the appearance of holes. If you decide to do this, work one extra decrease.

Change to US size 5 (3.75mm) needles and B.

Round 1 *K1, K2tog tbl, K to 3 sts before marker, K2tog, K1; rep from * once more.

Round 2 K.

Rep rounds 1 and 2 until 16 sts rem.

Distribute sts evenly over 2 needles, and graft together using Kitchener stitch.

To make the right sock

Work as for Left sock to **.

Using contrasting waste yarn, K24.

Slip next 24 sts and place marker to marker beg of round.

Pick up A and knit the 24 sts worked in waste yarn, then K to end of round.

Using A, K 3 rounds, making first and last sts slightly tighter to prevent holes.

Complete as given for Left Sock.

To finish

Weave in any loose yarn ends.

Gently steam the socks on the reverse to enhance the yarn.

13 Fanø Mittens

Influences from traditional Scandinavian designs and especially from the beautiful Danish island of Fanø are mixed up here in these fingerless mittens. They are worked in four colors with a beautiful super-fine wool-alpaca yarn on two needles.

Skill level

⬤⬛⬛▬
EXPERIENCED

In this project you will learn...
Working with two colors in a row using the stranding technique (see pages 28–30); working from a chart

Stitches used
Stockinette stitch

Materials
Super-fine-weight wool-alpaca yarn, such as
  Isager *Alpaca 2* (50% merino lambswool,
  50% baby alpaca; 270yd/247m per 1¾oz/50g
  hank; (**1**) SUPER FINE) in the following 4 colors:
    A raspberry (shade 17)—1 hank
    B dark blue gray (shade 47)—1 hank
    C pale blue (shade 4s)—1 hank
    D dusky plum (shade 52)—1 hank
Pair of US size 3 (3mm) knitting needles
Large blunt-tipped sewing needle

Size
One size to fit average woman's hand
Length from cuff edge to top edge 8¾in (22cm)

Gauge
38 sts and 36 rows to 4in (10cm) square measured over color pattern using US size 3 (3mm) needles. Use smaller or larger needles if necessary to obtain the correct gauge.

Abbreviations
Pm place marker (loop a piece of contrasting yarn, or a stitch marker, onto the needle or ends of row)
See also page 143.

Notes
Working the left and right mittens
Instructions are given for the left mitten. Instructions for right mitten follow in parentheses.

Working from the charts
When working the stockinette stitch color pattern from the charts using the stranding technique, read the right-side (knit) rows from right to left and the wrong-side (purl) rows from left to right.

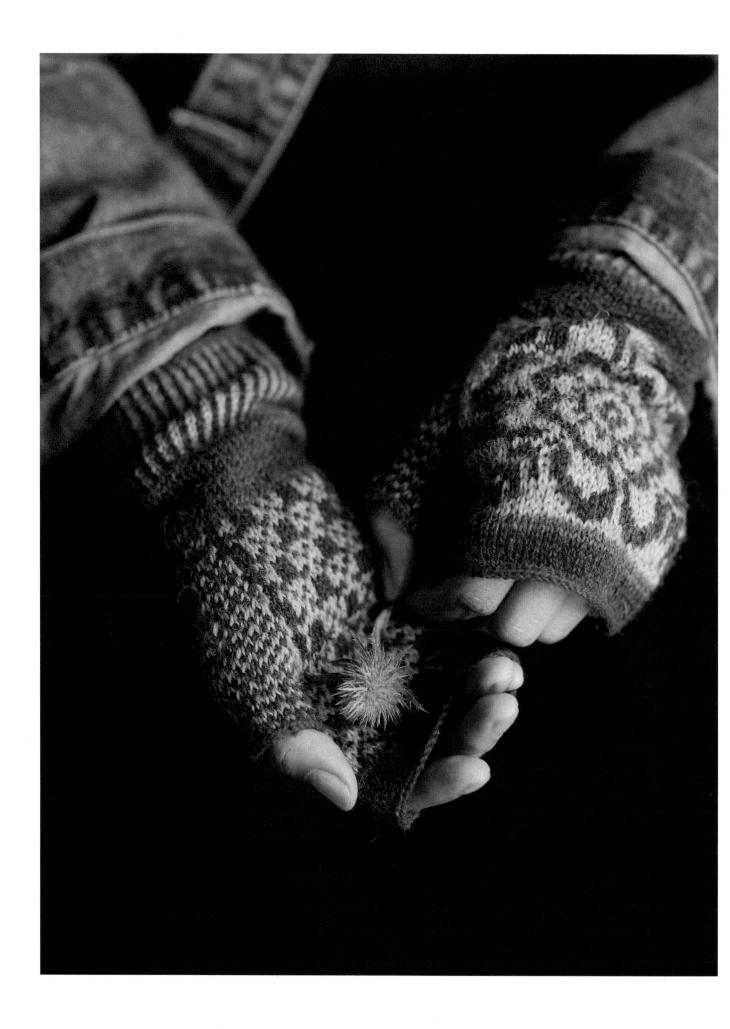

To make the mittens

Using A, cast on 70(70) sts.

Change to B and C and beg working in St st throughout as follows:

Row 1 (RS) *K1B, K1C; rep from * to end of row.

Row 2 *P1C, P1B; rep from * to end of row.

Rep last 2 rows until work measures 2¹⁄₂in (6.5cm) from cast-on edge, ending with RS facing for next row.

Change to D and work 2 rows St st.

Change to A and B and work checkerboard patt in St st as follows:

Next row (RS) *K1A, K1B; rep from * to end of row.

Next row *P1B, P1A; rep from * to end of row.

Rep last 2 rows 3 times more, so ending with RS facing for next row. *8 rows worked in total in checkerboard patt.*

Change to D and work 2 rows St st, so ending with RS facing for next row.

Shape thumb gusset

Using B and C, beg working the St st color pattern from the flower and plaid charts and start the gusset for the left(right) mitten as follows:

Row 1 (RS) K last 0(2) sts of row 1 of plaid chart, then K first 28(35) sts of row 1 of plaid(flower) chart; pm, K1B, M1, K1B, K1C, K1B, M1, K1B, pm (row 1 of thumb gusset); K last 2(0) sts of row 1 of plaid chart, then K first 35 (28) sts of row 1 of flower(plaid) chart.

Row 2 P first 35 (last 28) sts of row 2 of flower (plaid) chart, P first 2(0) sts of row 2 of plaid chart; slip marker onto right needle, P2B, P1C, P1B, P1C, P2B (row 2 of thumb gusset), slip second marker onto right needle; P last 28 (first 35) sts of row 2 of plaid(flower) chart.

The last 2 rows set the positions of the charts and the checkerboard thumb gusset.

Cont as set in chart patterns until chart row 18 has been completed **and at the same time** inc one st at each side of thumb gusset (as set in row 1) on third row and every foll alt row until there are 21 gusset sts between the markers (keeping checkerboard patt correct), ending with RS facing for next row. *86 sts.*

Work top of thumb

Row 19 (RS) Patt to the second marker, remove marker, TURN and cast on 3 sts, work in checkerboard patt to rem marker, remove marker, TURN and cast on 3 sts. *27 sts for thumb.*

Work 7 rows more in checkerboard patt on these 27 sts, so ending with WS facing for next row.

Change to A.

Next row P.

Bind off using A.

Sew thumb seam using mattress st.

With RS facing, rejoin C at base of thumb and pick up and K 5 sts from base of thumb, then patt to end of row 19. *70 sts.*

Now working all sts in patt, cont until row 36 of chart has been completed, so ending with RS facing for next row.

Change to D and work 2 rows in St st.

Change to B and work 4 rows in St st.

Change to A and work 2 rows in St st.

Bind off using A.

To finish

Weave in any loose yarn ends.

Gently steam the mittens on the reverse to enhance the yarn.

Sew the side seams using mattress stitch.

Flower chart

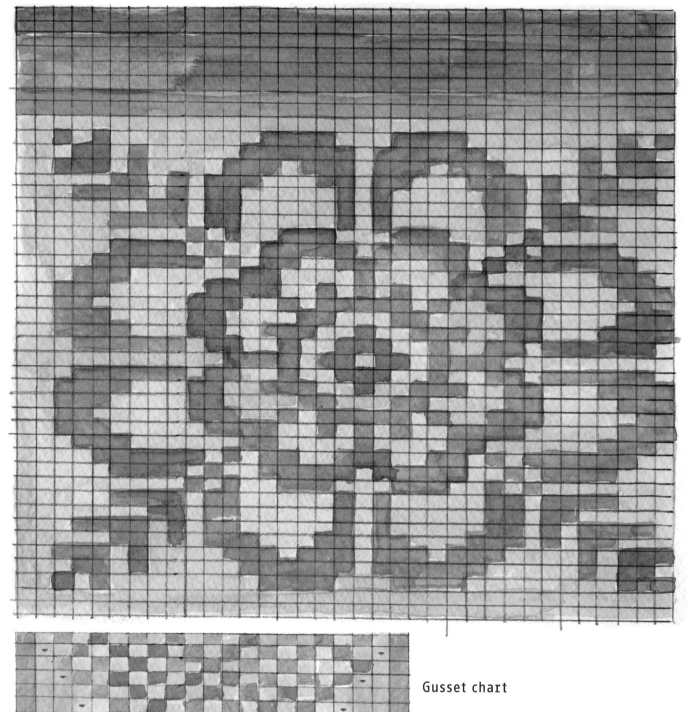

Gusset chart

Note Not all the squares on the gusset chart represent stitches, so follow the instructions on page 109 for shaping the gusset, referring to the chart for the positioning of the checkerboard pattern only. Note that the first and last stitch of the gusset on all rows is worked in B.

Plaid chart

43
41
39
37
35
33
31
29
27
25
23
21
19
17
15
13
11
9
7
5
3
1

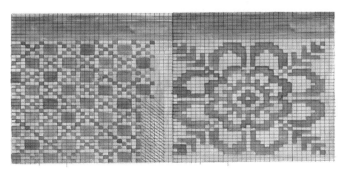

Positions of charts on right mitten

- ▨ A
- ▨ B
- ▢ C
- ▨ gusset position
- ▨ increases on gusset
- ▨ D

14 Color Wheel Pillow

A little parody of the ubiquitous color wheel found in every color theory book, this round pillow is worked in stockinette stitch in a linen-cotton yarn. The shape is created by the clever, simple short-row shaping technique.

Skill level

EASY

In this project you will learn...
Simple color blocking; short-row shaping

Stitches used
Stockinette stitch

Materials
Double-knitting-weight linen-cotton yarn, such as
  Rowan *Creative Linen* (50% linen, 50% cotton;
  219yd/200m per 3½oz/100g hank; **3** LIGHT)
  in the following 8 colors:
    A dark maroon (Eggplant 638)—1 hank
    B maroon red (Coleus 637)—1 hank
    C pale brown (Beige 622)—1 hank
    D light green (Apple 629)—1 hank
    E olive green (Leaf 632)—1 hank
    F light teal blue (Teal 625)—1 hank
    G light denim blue (Denim 630)—1 hank
    H dark steel blue (Stormy 635)—1 hank
Pair of US size 7 (4.5mm) knitting needles
Large blunt-tipped sewing needle
Round feather pillow form, approximately 16in
  (40cm) in diameter to fit finished cover

Size
Approximately 16in (40cm) in diameter

Gauge
21 sts and 30 rows to 4in (10cm) square measured over St st using US size 7 (4.5mm) needles. Use smaller or larger needles as necessary to obtain the correct the gauge.

Abbreviations
See page 143.

Note
Short-row shaping
For the short-row shaping, when the instructions say "TURN" at the end of the row, this means that the remaining stitches are not worked. To avoid creating a hole when turning on a knit row, work a wrap stitch—knit as far as instructed, then slip the next stitch purlwise onto the right-hand needle, bring the yarn forward between the two needles, slip the stitch back to the left-hand needle and take the yarn to the back between the two needles, turn, and purl to the end of the next row as instructed.

Color sequence for pillow-cover top

A
B
C
D
E
F
G
H

Color sequence for pillow-cover base

H
G
F
E
D
C
B
A

To make the pillow-cover top
Using A, cast on 42 sts.
**Work in St st and short rows as follows:
Row 1 K.
Row 2 P.
Row 3 K to last 2 sts, turn (see Note on page 112 on how to "turn" in short-row shaping).
Row 4 P.
Row 5 K to last 4 sts, turn.
Row 6 P.

Continue working in short rows as set, leaving 2 stitches more unworked on every knit row until there are no more stitches to knit.**
This completes the first color segment of the circle.
Change to B and rep from ** to ** for next color segment.
Continue repeating from ** to ** for each color segment until 8 segments have been worked to form a full circle, following the color sequence for the pillow-cover top.
Do not bind off stitches, but join last segment to first segment by grafting one stitch from needle with corresponding stitch on cast-on edge.

To make the pillow-cover base
Work as given for pillow-cover top, but cast on with H and use color sequence for the pillow-cover base.

To finish
Weave in any loose yarn ends.
Lay the work out flat and gently steam on the reverse to enhance the yarn.
Using a length of yarn and a blunt-tipped sewing needle, gently gather together the small hole in the center of each piece and fasten securely.
Sew the top and base pieces together, matching the colors along the seam and leaving an opening for inserting the pillow form. Insert the pillow form and sew the opening closed.

Geometric
Patchwork Throw

Knitted using the simple color block technique, this strong graphic patchwork-effect throw has unfinished cast-on, bound-off, and side edges for a contemporary detail. It is made in a luxuriously soft merino and mohair blend for ultimate coziness.

Skill level

INTERMEDIATE

In this project you will learn...
Color blocking (intarsia) technique (see page 32)

Stitches used...
Stockinette stitch

Materials
Bulky-weight wool-mohair yarn, such as Rowan *Cocoon* (80% merino wool, 20% kid mohair; 126yd/115m per 3½oz/100g ball; **5** BULKY) in the following 5 colors:

    A blue-green (Seascape 813)—3 balls
    B charcoal (Mountain 805)—3 balls
    C medium gray (Shale 804)—3 balls
    D light gray (Scree 803)—3 balls
    E pale gray (Alpine 802)—3 balls

US size 10½ (7mm) circular knitting needle, 40in (100cm) long and with a wire strong enough to take the weight of the project
Large blunt-tipped sewing needle

Size
Approximately 48in x 65in (120cm x 162.5cm)

Gauge
14 sts and 16 rows to 4in (10cm) square measured over St st using US size 10½ (7mm) needles. Use larger or smaller needles if necessary to obtain the correct gauge.

Abbreviations
See page 143.

Note
Working the color pattern
Work each triangle with a separate small ball of yarn, and when changing colors twist the yarns at back of work to avoid a hole.

To make the throw
Using the knit cast-on, cast-on 168 sts, joining in colors as follows—27D, 1B, 1D, 27C, 27A, 1E, 1B, 27C, 27A, 1D, 1C, 27E.

Rectangles row 1
With same side of work still facing, beg patt as follows:
Row 1 (RS) K across row, using colors for the triangles with right-leaning and left-leaning diagonals in chart row 1 as follows—27E, 1C, 1D, 27A, 27C, 1B, 1E, 27A, 27C, 1D, 1B, 27D.
Row 2 (WS) P across row, using colors for chart row 2 as follows—26D, 2B, 2D, 26C, 26A, 2E, 2B, 26C, 26A, 2D, 2C, 26E.
This sets the positions of the first row of two-color rectangles.
Cont in St st color patt as set until chart row 52 has been completed, so ending with RS facing for next row.

Rectangles rows 2–5
Work rectangles rows 2–5 following the color sequences diagram and the color chart, ending with chart row 51 on the last row of rectangles. Bind off purlwise, using the colors as set on chart row 52.

To finish
Weave in any loose yarn ends.
Gently steam on the reverse to enhance the yarn.

⊡ triangle one
⊠ triangle two

Note *The chart shows the 26-st rectangle with the right-leaning diagonal; for this rectangle, read the right-side (knit) rows from right to left and the wrong-side (purl) rows from left to right. For the rectangles with the left-leaning diagonal, the chart is flopped horizontally, so to do this read the right-side (knit) rows from left to right and the wrong-side (purl) rows from right to left.*

Color Sequences

The color sequences for each row of two-color 28-st rectangles are given below from left to right, but remember that when knitting the first row of each row of rectangles, you will be introducing the colors from right to left.

A blue-green
B charcoal
C medium gray
D light gray
E pale gray

patt repeat = 28 sts

Rectangles row 5 C/A, E/A, D/C, A/B, A/D, E/B

Rectangles row 4 E/C, A/B, E/D, A/E, C/A, B/C

Rectangles row 3 B/D, E/C, B/A, C/A, B/D, E/A

Rectangles row 2 A/C, E/A, C/D, A/D, C/E, B/D

Rectangles row 1 D/B, D/C, A/E, B/C, A/D, C/E

16 Squares Pillow

Backed with a printed cotton fabric, this pillow has a simple squares within squares color pattern made with the color-block (intarsia) technique. Play with tonal colors or experiment with opposites to create a personal statement.

Skill level

⬛⬛⬛▢

INTERMEDIATE

In this project you will learn...
Color-blocking (intarsia) technique (see page 32); reading from a chart

Stitches used...
Stockinette stitch

Materials
Double-knitting-weight wool yarn, such as Erika
  Knight *British Blue Wool* (100% Blue-Faced
  Leicester wool; 60yd/55m per ¾oz/25g ball;
  (3) LIGHT) in the following 6 colors:
    A pink (Boho 048)—1 ball
    B pale beige (Fawn 037)—2 balls
    C purple (French 043)—2 balls
    D gray (Mouse 039)—1 ball
    E brown (Milk Chocolate 044)—1 ball
    F light blue (Iced Gem 041)—1 ball
Pair of US size 5 (3.75mm) knitting needles
Large blunt-tipped sewing needle
1½yd (50cm) of a cotton fabric print, for back
Sewing needle and matching sewing thread, for
  fabric back
Square feather pillow form, 16in x 16in
  (40cm x 40cm)

Note: Yarn amounts given are based on average requirements and are approximate.

Size
Approximately 16in x 16in (40cm x 40cm)

Gauge
22 sts and 30 rows to 4in (10cm) square measured over St st using US size 5 (3.75mm) needles. Use larger or smaller needles if necessary to obtain the correct gauge.

Abbreviations
See page 143.

Notes
Working the color pattern
Using the color-blocking (intarsia) technique, work each area of color with a separate small ball of yarn, and when changing colors twist the yarns at back of work to avoid a hole.

Working from the chart
The large square on the chart is 29 stitches wide and 40 rows tall, and the smaller inner square is 9 stitches wide by 13 rows tall. When working from the chart, read all odd-numbered (knit) rows from right to left and all even-numbered (purl) rows from left to right.

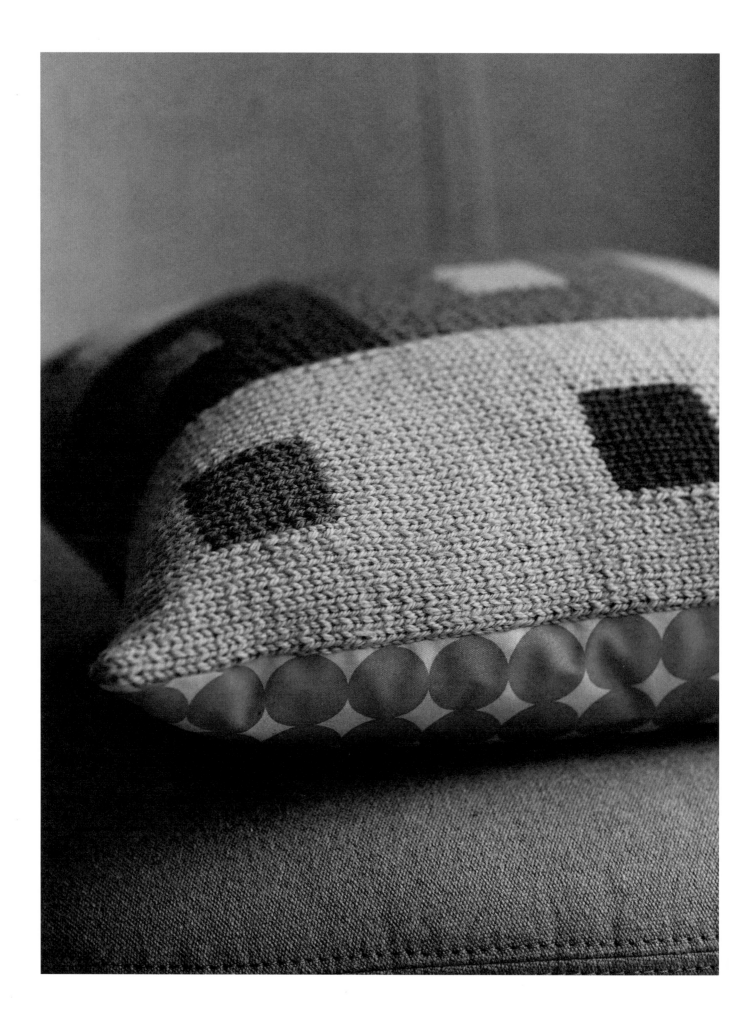

To make the pillow-cover front

Using the knit cast-on, cast on 87 sts, joining in colors as follows—29C, 29B, 29A.

Squares row 1

With same side of work still facing, beg patt as follows:

Row 1 (RS) K across row, using colors for the squares in chart row 1 as follows—29A, 29B, 29C.

Row 2 P across row, using colors for chart row 2 as follows—29C, 29B, 29A.

Rows 3–12 [Rep rows 1 and 2] 5 times.

Row 13 Rep row 1.

Row 14 P across row, using colors as follows—10C, 9E, 10C, 10B, 9D, 10B, 10A, 9C, 10A.

Row 15 K across row, using colors as follows—10A, 9C, 10A, 10B, 9D, 10B, 10C, 9E, 10C.

Rows 16–25 [Rep rows 14 and 15] 5 times.

Row 26 Rep row 14.

Rows 27–40 [Rep rows 1 and 2] 7 times.

This completes the first row of two-color squares, so ending with RS facing for next row.

Squares rows 2 and 3

Following the chart, work squares rows 2 and 3 as set, but following the color diagram for colors. Bind off purlwise, using the same colors as the last row.

To finish the pillow-cover front

Weave in any loose yarn ends.

Lay the work out flat and gently steam on the reverse to enhance the yarn.

To add the fabric pillow cover back

Cut a piece of fabric the same size as the knitted front plus 1/2in (1.5cm) extra all around for the seam allowance.

With right sides together, pin the pillow-cover front to the fabric along the seam lines, easing to fit. Using matching thread and a sewing needle, stitch the knitted front to the fabric back piece around three sides.

Turn the pillow cover right side out. Insert the pillow form and sew the remaining side closed.

patt repeat = 29 sts

☐ background color

☒ center square color

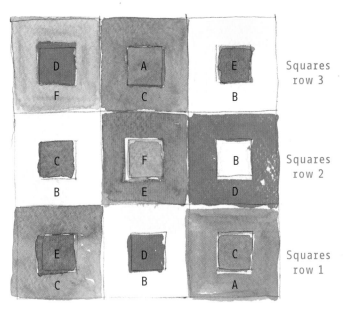

Squares row 3

Squares row 2

Squares row 1

17 Spots Pillows

The spots are worked on a light background on one of these two pillows and the other uses exactly the same colors but has a dark background—a simple color trick that always works. The beautiful wool-silk yarn not only takes color well but gives great stitch definition.

Skill level

■■■□
INTERMEDIATE

In this project you will learn...
Color-blocking (intarsia) technique (see page 32); reading from a chart

Stitches used...
Stockinette stitch

Materials
For both pillows
Super-fine-weight wool-silk yarn, such as Shibui *Staccato* (70% superwash merino wool, 30% silk; 191yd/175m per 1¾oz/50g hank; ① SUPER FINE) in the following 4 colors:
    A light silvery gray (Ash 2003)—2 hanks
    B deep dusky plum (Velvet 2017)—1 hank
    C dark rich brown (Grounds 2025)—2 hanks
    D medium brown-gray (Mineral 2022)—1 hank
Pair of US size 2 (2.75mm) knitting needles
Large blunt-tipped sewing needle
½yd (50cm) of a plain shiny fabric, for each back
Sewing needle and matching sewing thread, for fabric back
Two square feather pillow forms, 13in x 13in (32cm x 32cm)

Note: Yarn amounts given are based on average requirements and are approximate.

Size
Each pillow measures approximately 13in x 13in (32cm x 32cm)

Gauge
28 sts and 38 rows to 4in (10cm) square measured over St st using US size 2 (2.75mm) needles. Use larger or smaller needles if necessary to obtain the correct gauge.

Abbreviations
See page 143.

Notes
Working the color pattern
Using the color-blocking (intarsia) technique, work each area of color with a separate small ball of yarn, and when changing colors twist the yarns at back of work to avoid a hole.

Working from the chart
When working from the chart, read all odd-numbered (knit) rows from right to left and all even-numbered (purl) rows from left to right.

To make the pillow-cover front
Follow the first color for the light version and the color in parentheses for the dark version.
Using A(C), cast on 90 sts.
Beg with a K row, work 6 rows in St st, so ending RS facing for next row.
Place the first row of spots on the next row as follows:
Row 7 (RS) K12A(C), yf, P6A(C), yb, K24A(C), K6D(D), K24A(C), K6B(B), K12A(C). *90 sts*.
Row 8 P10A(C), P8B(B), P20A(C), P8D(D), P20A(C), yb, K8A(C), yf, P10A(C). *90 sts*.
Cont in St st, following the chart for the colored spots and the rev St st textured spots, until chart row 114 has been completed.
Bind off in A(C).

To finish the pillow-cover front
Weave in any loose yarn ends.
Lay the work out flat and gently steam on the reverse to enhance the yarn.

To add the fabric pillow-cover back
Cut a piece of fabric the same size as the knitted front plus 1/2in (1.5cm) extra all around for the seam allowance.
With right sides together, pin the pillow-cover front to the fabric along the seam lines, easing to fit. Using matching thread and a sewing needle, stitch the knitted front to the fabric back piece around three sides.
Turn the pillow cover right side out. Insert the pillow form and sew the remaining side closed.

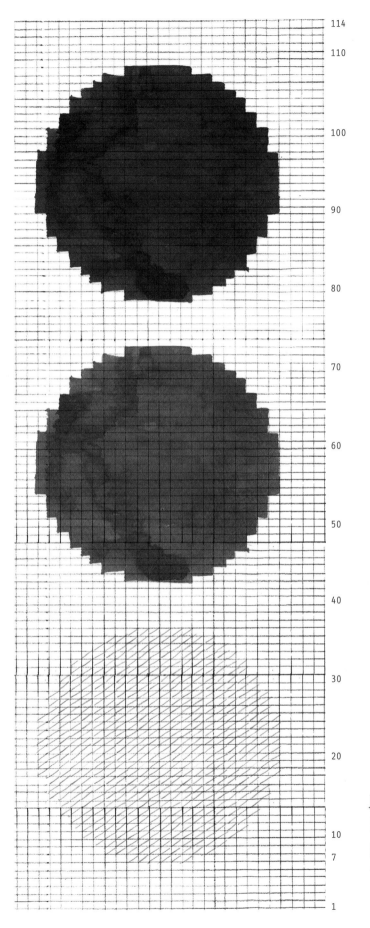

114
110

100

90

80

70

60

50

40

30

20

10
7

1

Light version **Dark version**

A *in St st*   C *in St st*

A *in rev St st*   C *in rev St st*

B *in St st*   B *in St st*

C *in St st*   A *in St st*

D *in St st*   D *in St st*

18 Spotty Blanket

Worked in three colors using the double-knitting technique, this spot pattern creates a contemporary reversible baby blanket. The instructions are for a back and front in the same pattern in reversed colors, but feel free to vary the pattern on the back like I did.

Skill level

EXPERIENCED

In this project you will learn...
Double-knitting technique; working from a chart

Stitches used...
Stockinette stitch

Materials
Double-knitting-weight wool yarn, such as Erika Knight *British Blue Wool* (100% Blue-Faced Leicester wool; 60yd/55m per ¾oz/25g ball; **3** LIGHT) in the following 3 colors:
- A red (Mysore Red 051)—6 balls
- B pale green (Leaf 045)—5 balls
- C gray (Mouse 039)—7 balls
US size 6 (4mm) circular knitting needle, 40in (100cm) long
Large blunt-tipped sewing needle

Note: Yarn amounts given are based on average requirements and are approximate.

Size
Approximately 22¾in x 21¼in (57cm x 53cm)

Gauge
20 sts and 26 rows to 4in (10cm) square measured over double-knit St st using US size 6 (4mm) needles. Use larger or smaller needles if necessary to obtain the correct gauge.

Abbreviations
See page 143.

Note
Working the double-knitting fabric
The double-knitting technique creates two layers of stockinette stitch fabric situated back to back with their wrong or purl sides facing each other and their right or knit sides facing out. The two pieces are connected at the cast-on edge and the sides but entirely separate throughout the center, just like two sides of a pocket.
When the fabric is a solid color one ball of yarn is used for each layer, and for the 2-color Fair Isle rows two balls are used for each layer.
This double fabric must be worked on a circular knitting needle (or double-pointed needles) as the work is not turned on the first row and the following alternate rows, but worked a second time in the same direction.
When turning the work, make sure the yarns are twisted around each other.

Slipping stitches on double-knitting
Slip all stitches purlwise.

To make the throw
Using C, cast on 228 sts—this will provide 114 sts for each side of the double fabric.
Begin the double-knitting, working each row twice in the same direction as follows:
Row 1a (front of fabric facing) Using A, *K1, yf, sl 1, yb; rep from * to end—slide sts back to other end of needle without turning work and beg next row with same side facing.
112 sts each side.
Row 1b (front of fabric facing) Using C, *yb, sl 1, yf, P1; rep from * to end—TURN work.
Row 2a (back of fabric facing) Using A, rep row 2—slide sts back to other end of needle without

turning work and beg next row with same side facing.

Row 2b (back of fabric facing) Using C, rep row 1—TURN work.

This completes the first 2 St st rows of the front layer in A and the first 2 St st rows of back layer in C, called "2 rows A(C)"—where A is the color used for the front layer and C the color used for the back layer.

Working 2 rows with the front of the fabric facing and 2 rows with the back of the work facing as set throughout, cont to form the St st stripe and spots pattern in reverse colors on the front and back as follows:

6 rows more A(C).

8 rows of small C(A) spots on A(C) background, following chart rows 2–9 and working any sts left after the 12th spot in background color.

2 rows A(C).

2 rows B(C).

8 rows of small C(B) spots on B(C) background.

2 rows B(C).

22 rows A(C).

12 rows C(A).

2 rows A(C).

2 rows B(C).

10 rows of large C(B) spots on B(C) background, following chart rows 2–11 and working any sts left after the 10th spot in background color.

4 rows B(C).

8 rows of small C(B) spots on B(C) background.

2 rows B(C).

2 rows A(C).

8 rows C(A).

2 rows A(C).

2 rows B(C).

12 rows C(B)

2 rows B(C).

2 rows A(C).

8 rows of small C(A) spots on A(C) background.

8 rows A(C).

Using A, bind off 2 sts at a time, by knitting through one front st and one back st with each st.

To finish

Weave in any loose yarn ends.
Lay the work out flat and gently steam on the reverse to enhance the yarn.

Small spots chart

patt repeat = 9 sts

Large spots chart

patt repeat = 11 sts

19 Coffee Cup Cozy

In color blocking or "intarsia" a separate ball or bobbin of yarn is used for each area of color. This coffee cozy is a quick and easy project to try out this technique and also uses "cheat's" intarsia or duplicate stitch embroidery for the black lines.

Skill level

INTERMEDIATE

In the project you will learn...
Color-blocking (intarsia) technique; duplicate stitch embroidery

Stitches used
Stockinette stitch; K1, P1 rib

Materials
Aran-weight wool yarn, such as Erika Knight *Vintage Wool* (100% pure British wool; 95yd/87m per 1¾oz/50g hank; (4) MEDIUM) in the following 7 colors:
- A pale beige (Flax)—1 hank
- B gray (Drizzle)—1 hank
- C dark grape (Mulberry)—1 hank
- D aqua (Leighton)—1 hank
- E fuchsia (Gorgeous)—1 hank
- F dark blue (Dark)—1 hank
- G black (Pitch)—1 hank

Pair of US size 7 (4.5mm) knitting needles
Large blunt-tipped sewing needle

Size
To fit average-size "take out" paper coffee cup

Gauge
18½ sts and 26 rows to 4in (10cm) square measured over color pattern using US size 7 (4.5mm) needles. Use larger or smaller needles if necessary to obtain the correct gauge.

Abbreviations
See page 143.

Notes
Working from a chart
Work the diamonds color pattern in stockinette stitch following the chart (omitting the black rakers). Use the color-blocking (intarsia) technique and read odd-numbered (knit) chart rows from right to left and even-numbered (purl) chart rows from left to right. See page 32 for how to work color blocking.

Working the duplicate stitch embroidery
Use duplicate stitch to embroider the black "criss cross" or "rakers" onto the finished diamond pattern. See pages 34–35 for how to work duplicate stitch.

To make the cup cozy

Using A, cast on 42 sts.

Work 3 rows in K1, P1 rib.

Beg with a K row, work 2 rows in St st, so ending with RS facing for next row.

Using the intarsia method and six colors (A, B, C, D, E, and F), introduce chart patt on next rows as follows:

Row 1 (RS) K1A; K 40 sts of chart row 1 across next 40 sts as follows – 3A, 2F, 6A, 2E, 6A, 2D, 6A, 2C, 6A, 2B, 3A; K1A.

Row 2 P1A; P 40 sts of chart row 2 across next 40 sts as follows – 3A, 2B, 6A, 2C, 6A, 2D, 6A, 2E, 6A, 2F, 3A; P1A.

Last 2 rows set position of chart.

Cont diamond patt following rows 3–14 of chart **and at the same time** inc 1 st at each end of row 5 and row 11. *46 sts.*

Using A, work 2 rows in St st.

Work 3 rows in K1, P1 rib.

Bind off in rib.

To finish

Weave in any loose yarn ends.

Lay the work out flat and gently steam on the reverse to enhance the yarn, avoiding the ribbing.

Following the chart and using G (black), duplicate stitch the rakers across the diamonds.

Sew the side seam using an invisible stitch.

A *in St st*

B *in St st*

C *in St st*

D *in St st*

E *in St st*

F *in St st*

G *in duplicate stitch*

20 Plaid Rose Pillow

To add layers of pattern to your color knitting, simply select a bold fabric pattern, photocopy it, enlarge or reduce it to suit your design and trace it onto knitter's chart paper. Then work it and vertical stripes in duplicate stitch onto the knitting.

Skill level

INTERMEDIATE

In this project you will learn...
How to change colors; duplicate stitch embroidery

Stitches used...
Stockinette stitch

Materials
Fine-weight cotton yarn, such as Rowan *Cotton Glacé* (100% mercerized cotton; 125yd/115m per 1¾oz/50g ball; **2** FINE) in the following 10 colors:
    A bright pink (Bubbles 724)—2 balls
    B dark red (Blood Orange 445)—1 ball
    C plum (Garnet 841)—1 ball
    D light gray (Dawn Grey 831)—1 ball
    E bright yellow (Mineral 856)—1 ball
    F pale yellow (Ochre 833)—1 ball
    G pale orange (Persimmon 832)—1 ball
    H black (Black 727)—1 ball
    I pale green (Shoot 814)—1 ball
    J bright blue (Aqua 858)—1 ball
Pair of US size 5 (3.75mm) knitting needles
Large blunt-tipped sewing needle
½yd (50cm) of a cotton fabric print, for back
Sewing needle and matching sewing thread, for fabric back
Square feather pillow form, 18in x 18in (45cm x 45cm)

Note: Yarn amounts given are based on average requirements and are approximate.

Size
Approximately 17¾in x 17¾in (44.5cm x 44.5cm)

Gauge
21½ sts and 30 rows to 4in (10cm) measured over St st using US size 5 (3.75mm) needles. Use larger or smaller needles if necessary to obtain the correct gauge.

Abbreviations
See page 143.

Notes
Joining in a new color for stripes
On the row before you need the new color, work to the last stitch. Taking the end of the new color, use together with the yarn in work to work the last stitch, creating a "double stitch." On the first stitch of next row, work the double stitch as one stitch with just the end of the new color. This will securely "anchor" your new yarn and neither create unsightly knots nor create bumps.

Working the duplicate stitch embroidery
Use duplicate stitch to embroider the rose and leaves and the vertical lines onto the striped knitting. See pages 34–35 for how to work duplicate stitch.

To make the pillow-cover front

Using A, cast on 96 sts.
Beg with a K row, work in St st using the stripe sequence as follows:
A 10 rows
C 1 row
B 3 rows
A 30 rows
C 1 row
[B 1 row, C 1 row] 9 times
B 24 rows
A 11 rows
C 1 row
B 3 rows
A 30 rows
Bind off.

To embellish

Using the small chart, duplicate stitch the leaf motif, with the colors indicated, in the bottom left-hand corner of the knitting. Position the motif so that the first row of leaf stitches are 2 rows up from the bottom of the knitting and the leaf tip at the left edge is 2 stitches in from the left side edge of the knitting.

Using the big chart, duplicate stitch the rose and leavesmotif, with the colors indicated, at the top right-hand side of the knitting. Position the motif so that the tip of the top leaf is 2 rows down from the top edge of the knitting and the right edge of the motif is 2 stitches from the right side edge of the knitting.

Duplicate stitch the 2-stitch-wide vertical lines in J and D. Position the center vertical line 48 stitches in from right-hand edge, the left vertical line 16 sts in from left-hand edge (starting where the leaf finished), and the right vertical line 15 sts in from right-hand edge in the areas without the motif.

To finish the the pillow-cover front

Weave in any loose yarn ends.
Lay the work out flat and gently steam on the reverse to enhance the yarn.

To add the fabric pillow-cover back

Cut a piece of fabric the same size as the knitted front plus 1/2in (1.5cm) extra all around for the seam allowance.

With right sides together, pin the pillow-cover front to the fabric along the seam lines, easing to fit. Using matching thread and a sewing needle, stitch the knitted front to the fabric back piece around three sides.

Turn the pillow cover right side out. Insert the pillow form and sew the remaining side closed.

17¾in (44.5cm)

17¾in (44.5cm)

E   H

F   I

G   J

Recommended yarns

There is a yarn specified for each of the twenty designs in the Project Workshops section of this book. If you stick to the recommended yarn, you just need to pick your preferred shades. However, if you want to use a different yarn than the one specified, you need to compare the gauges given to ensure the finished result will not differ too wildly.

There are standard weights—or thicknesses—of yarns, recognized throughout the spinner's industry. Hand-knit yarns commonly range from lace yarn and fingering through sport and worsted to super bulky at the opposite end of the scale. Within each of these categories there is a degree of tolerance, so it is still important to check the gauge of each yarn against that given in a pattern. The weight categories listed with the yarns for the projects (1 super fine, 2 fine, 3 light, 4 medium, 5 bulky, and 6 super bulky) have been determined by the weight categories recognized by the Craft Yarn Council of America. If using a substitute yarn, use these categories as a helpful guide.

Each yarn will have slightly varying physical properties from the next and will perform differently. Some yarns may be colorfast and easycare while others may only be suitable for dry-cleaning or could possibly felt if not treated correctly. The care information for a yarn will be given on the yarn label that comes with the yarn—it is either a paper band wrapped around the ball, skein, or hank, or a paper tag tied to the yarn. I always keep a yarn label for each project that I make—and if I give a hand knit as a gift, I include the yarn label so the recipient knows how to care for the item. When you invest so much of your time and energy into creating a hand-knitted item, great care should be taken in the laundering.

Alongside the manufacturer's brand name and the name given to the specific yarn, a yarn label will typically carry the following information:

Average gauge and recommended needle sizes
This is the spinner's recommended gauge and needle size. A designer may vary from this recommendation within a pattern. If so, always go with the designer's recommendation.

Weight of yarn balls and hanks
Most yarns come in either 1¾-ounce (50-gram) or 3½-ounce (100-gram) balls or hanks.

Yardage (meterage)
This is the length of yarn in the ball and is just as important to consider as gauge when purchasing a substitute yarn. Always purchase a substitute yarn by how many yards (meters) you need rather than by how many ounces (grams).

Fiber composition
A yarn label will list the materials that the yarn is made from, whether that is 100% pure wool or a blend of fibers such as cotton and silk. This affects not just the method of care for the finished item, but also the suitability of a yarn for a certain project.

Shade and dye-lot numbers
Each shade of yarn is given an identifying name and/or number by the manufacturer. When purchasing yarn the dye-lot number is equally, if not more important, as this number needs to be the same on every ball. As yarn is dyed in batches, buying yarn with the same dye-lot numbers ensures there will be no color variations between balls.

Care instructions
A yarn label will indicate whether the yarn is suitable for machine washing or is dry-clean only, and whether or not it can be ironed and, if so, at what temperature. This information is usually given in the form of standard fabric-care symbols.

The following are the specifications for all the yarns used in this book:

Erika Knight *British Blue Wool* (3) LIGHT
A double-knitting-weight wool yarn; 100% Blue-Faced Leicester wool; 60yd/55m per ¾oz/25g; 22 sts sts x 30 rows per 4in/10cm over St st using US size 6 (4mm) needles.

Erika Knight *Fur Wool* (6) SUPER BULKY
A super-bulky-weight wool "fur" yarn; 97% wool, 3% nylon binder; 44yd/40m per 3½oz/100g hank; 5½ sts x 8 rows per 4in/10cm over St st using US size 19 (15mm) needles.

Erika Knight *Maxi Wool* (6) SUPER BULKY
A super-bulky-weight wool yarn; 100% British wool; 87yd/80m per 3½oz/100g hank; 8 sts x 12 rows per 4in/10cm over St st using US size 17 (12mm) needles.

Erika Knight *Vintage Wool* (4) MEDIUM
An Aran-weight wool yarn; 100% British wool; 95yd/87m per 1¾oz/50g hank; 18 sts x 24 rows per 4in/10cm over St st using US size 8 (5mm) needles.

Isager *Alpaca 2* (1) SUPER FINE
A super-fine-weight wool-alpaca yarn; 50% merino lambswool, 50% baby alpaca; 270yd/247m per 1¾oz/50g; 26 sts rows per 4in/10cm over St st using US size 3 (3mm) needles.

Lana Knits *Allhemp6* (3) LIGHT
A double-knitting-weight hemp yarn; 100% hemp; 165yd/150m per 3½oz/100g hank; 22 sts per 4in/10cm over St st using US size 5 (3.75mm) needles.

Knitting abbreviations

Madeline Tosh *Tosh DK* (3) LIGHT
A double-knitting-weight hand-dyed wool yarn; 100% superwash merino wool; 225yd/206m per 3½oz/100g hank; 20–22 sts per 4in/10cm over St st using US size 6–7 (4–4.5mm) needles.

Rowan *Cocoon* (5) BULKY
A bulky-weight wool-mohair yarn; 80% merino wool, 20% kid mohair; 126yd/115m per 3½oz/100g ball; 14 sts x 16 rows per 4in/10cm over St st using US size 10½ (7mm) needles.

Rowan *Cotton Glacé* (2) FINE
A fine-weight cotton yarn; 100% mercerized cotton; 125yd/115m per 1¾oz/50g ball; 23 sts x 32 rows per 4in/10cm over St st using US size 3 (3.25mm) needles.

Rowan *Creative Linen* (3) LIGHT
A double-knitting-weight linen-cotton yarn; 50% linen, 50% cotton; 219yd/200m per 3½oz/100g hank; 21 sts x 28 rows per 4in/10cm over St st using US size 7 (4.5mm) needles.

Shibui *Staccato* (1) SUPER FINE
A super-fine-weight wool-silk yarn; 70% superwash merino wool, 30% silk; 191yd/175m per 1¾oz/50g hank; 28–32 sts per 4in/10cm over St st using US size 1–2 (2.25–2.75mm) needles.

Knitting needle sizes
The closest equivalent sizes across three needle-sizing systems—UK metric, US and old UK (imperial) follow.

Metric	US	Old UK	Metric	US	Old UK
15mm	19	–	4.5mm	7	7
12mm	17	–	4mm	6	8
10mm	15	000	3.75mm	5	9
9mm	13	00	3.5mm	4	–
8mm	11	0	3.25mm	3	10
7.5mm	–	1	3mm	–	11
7mm	–	2	2.75mm	2	12
6.5mm	10½	3	2.5mm	–	–
6mm	10	4	2.25mm	1	13
5.5mm	9	5	2mm	0	14
5mm	8	6			

The following are the abbreviations used in this book. Any special abbreviations are given with individual patterns.

alt	alternate
beg	begin(ning)
cm	centimetre(s)
cont	continu(e)(ing)
dec	decreas(e)(ing)
foll	follow(s)(ing)
g	gram(s)
in	inch(es)
inc	increas(e)(ing)
K	knit
m	metre(s)
M1	make one st; pick up strand between st just knit and next st with tip of left needle and work into back of it (to increase 1 st)
mm	millimetre(s)
oz	ounce(s)
P	purl
patt	pattern; or work in pattern
psso	pass slipped stitch over
rem	remain(s)(ing)
rep	repeat(s)(ing)
rev St st	reverse stockinette stitch
RS	right side
sl	slip
st(s)	stitch(es)
St st	stockinette stitch
tbl	through back of loop(s)
tog	together
WS	wrong side
yb	yarn to back of work between two needles
yd	yard(s)
yf	yarn to front of work between two needles
* [ ]	Repeat instructions after asterisk, between asterisks, or inside brackets as many times as instructed.

Acknowledgments

Simple Color Knitting has been a long time in the making, a somewhat elongated journey, with many bumps and detours along the way, which have altered, refined, and framed the final product. Color is a constant journey, it refreshes ones creative spirit like nothing else, always changing with light, space, and mood. Color is intrinsic to who we are and to how we interpret our environment. Color is the inspiration and stimulus to my personal creative process and the journey of putting this book together has indeed been a colorful one.

It has involved the very best people of the highest caliber with the most discerning eyes, exacting standards, meticulous attention to detail, and most of all unbelievable patience in working with me. For all of which I am enormously grateful and I would like to extend my heartfelt thanks and appreciation for their huge contributions. It is a privilege to work with all of them and most certainly this book would not have happened without them.

I am forever appreciative of my long association with Quadrille Publishing. And most especially with Jane O'Shea, my publishing director, who since the beginning has championed me. No one has the ability to chastise and encourage with such style. I have tried and challenged the patience of my creative editor Lisa Pendreigh beyond question and her professionalism, unwavering support, innate creative talents, perception, and perseverance is faultless. She is simply the best. Vast thanks to Claire Peters, for surpassing my vision of the concept for this book, with her creative design and glorious watercolor illustrations. And to Vincent Smith and his team for the exceptional production.

I am indebted to Sally Harding for her huge contribution to this book, for her inestimable and meticulous endeavor in checking the patterns and text. She is a one-stop shop for all things knit and crochet and thank goodness for that.

I am thrilled to have Yuki Sugiura to photograph the book, her innate yet ease of style is inherent to the sensibility of this book, and of course huge thanks to Kim Lightbody for assisting. It was fabulous to have stylist Holly Bruce, a whirlwind of enthusiasm and energy to collate and create for us. Chinh Hoang, huge thanks for being so elegantly and effortlessly beautiful. Sincerest thanks to Simon Kämpfer, a hugely talented designer of exquisite furniture, who went the extra mile so we would have the most beautiful pieces which elevated the projects far beyond the humble handmade, and to Simon's studio for loaning the pieces.

Enduring gratitude and thanks to Sally Lee, my creative practitioner, for her immense contribution to this book, her expertise, diligence, and pragmatism are rare and greatly appreciated. And to a small but perfectly selected team of design sample knitters and makers, most especially Faye Perriam, Jools Yeo, Eileen Maccabe, and Lucyna Coyne. And to Amelia Bur who made invaluable contributions during her internship with me.

To Kate Buller of Rowan Yarns, Amy Hendrix of MadeleineTosh, Darcy Cameron of Shibui, Lana Hames of LanaKnits, and Isager, my huge thanks for creating inspirational and exceptional yarns of the highest quality and, invaluably, for their generosity in contributing yarns for the projects and support of this book.

Finally and fundamentally to Bella, my daughter, and now collaborator in the Erika Knight Yarn Collection. She has always said, "It's in her genes." I have no words (for once) to express my thanks, appreciation, gratitude, and respect in all that she is, what she does for me, and getting us here.

And finally this book is dedicated to those who love color and creating and CRAFT.

Publisher's Acknowledgments
The publisher would like to thank the following for loaning accessories and other items:

BRICKETT DAVDA
www.brickettdavda.com
The yarn bowls on page 112 are made by Brickett Davda exclusively for Erika Knight. For further information, contact info@erikaknight.co.uk.

DE LA ESPADA
www.delaespada.com

SIMON KÄMPFER
www.simonkaempfer.com

VOLGA LINEN
www.volgalinen.co.uk